The BottleHopper

Surviving Ethyl Alcohol

By Bob Edwards

eShore

Imprint of SterlingHouse Publisher, Inc.

Pittsburgh, PA

ISBN 1-58501-031-6

Trade Paperback
©Copyright 2002 Bob Edwards
All rights reserved
First Printing—2002
Library of Congress #2001094627

Request for information should be addressed to:

CeShore
SterlingHouse Publisher, Inc.
7436 Washington Avenue
Suite 200
Pittsburgh, PA 15218
www.sterlinghousepublisher.com

CeShore is an imprint of SterlingHouse Publisher, Inc.
Cover Design: Jeffrey S. Butler—SterlingHouse Publisher
Book Design: Bernadette E. Kazmarski

This publication includes images from (Corel Draw 8) or
(Adobe 6.5) which are protected by the copyright laws of the
U.S., Canada and elsewhere.

Printed in The United States of America

DRUNK TANK 1
GO FOR THE GUSTO 7
THE ALCOHOLIC PERSONALITY 17
BIRCH BAY HERO 23
NORMAL DRINKING CANADIAN DUDE 29
RHAPSODY FOR ETHYL 37
BOB TURNS HIMSELF IN 42
STREET WISE 50
THE COMPLETE PREDATOR 57
ADVENTURES 64
SCHOOL DAYS 73
ZAPPED 78
FRASER HOUSE 85
HOT STUFF 93
ONE STEP BACK 99
STAYING COOL 105
OF SLIPS AND SLIDES 114
TRANSITIONS 122
GOOD THINGS HAPPEN TO GOOD PEOPLE 130
TALES OF THREE CHILDREN 137
AWARDS BANQUET 143
SUCCESS 153
UNIVERSITY LECTURE 159
YESTERDAY AND TODAY 168
AFTERWORD: FREQUENTLY ASKED QUESTIONS 173
KEEP GOING ON...GOING 182

Acknowledgements

Where to begin? So many involved. To Dr. Louis Pagliaro and Dr. Anne Marie Pagliaro (who is a lot prettier), thank you my friends for the idea and support during the creation of the manuscript. Dr. T.H. Maguire for keeping me alive. Thanks Tom. Paul Wood, my Maui editor for his encouragement and expertise. To Lee Shore Agency many thanks from one who had never dreamed of swimming in these unchartered waters of words. My publisher SterlingHouse and their dedicated team of professionals. Special thanks to Jennifer Himes and Jennifer Piemme. Good things do come in twos. My friends who encouraged me by saying the manuscript is going to be a very good book; Dr. J. Vandenbrink and staff, Sean Armstrong, Mac Tyler, Lana Irwin, Lori Cameron, Pat Hyde, Jeff Walter, Jim Carmichael, Dr. Maggie Kirchen, Jeromy Loome, Laura Wall, Vernon...so many more...Thanks.

Maui, December 11, 2001

Dedicated to

To my wife Pat and daughter Tricia, who supported me in relapse and actively participated in my recovery. Not to deride, not to pity, not to detest. Your striving to understand my addictions is reflected in the unconditional love I have for both of you. My Higher Power, who is omnipotent, and has a sense of humor, it's been a slice. To members of both 12 step programs, thanks, To the alcoholic-addict still out there struggling. THERE IS HOPE... For the rest of you, "Judge not lest you be judged..."

Kihei, Maui, December 12, 2001

Foreword

Hello, my name is Dr. Pagliaro and my clinical specialization is the assessment and treatment of individuals with dual diagnoses (i.e., an alcohol or other substance use disorder that co-exists with one or more additional mental disorders, such as an anxiety disorder or depression). It was in this capacity that I met first boB (Bob). Several years ago he was referred to me by a caring health care colleague whose treatment center had tried several times over as many years to help him, but had finally "given up". In fact, Bob told me, at the time, that they had a picture of him at the intake clinic for this public agency and were told *not* to admit him! You will soon find that Bob can tell his own story better than anyone else. Thus, I will make a few additional comments not about the specific events of his story, but about its nature and its theme.

We are all familiar with the old adage that "Hope springs eternal from the human breast." This is Bob's story. The story of a man who had it "all," who lost it "all," and who was able to get it "all back" through hope, determination, and hard work (with some obvious love and support from his family and friends).

*"**The Bottlehopper**"*, in today's parlance, is a "reality TV" look at the phenomenon of alcoholism. As such, it is bound to stir many deep and varied emotions for the reader. Upon reflection, I am reminded of the words of the philosopher, Spinoza, who provided us several hundred years ago with the following guidance that we may find of benefit when we read about the varied exploits of an alcoholic, who is a man, and of a man, who is an alcoholic:

"Not to deride, not to grieve, not to detest,
but to understand."

I trust that the reading of this book will provide you, the reader, with a much deeper and fuller understanding of alcoholism, of despair, and of the human capacity for hope and success.

Sincerely,

Dr. Louis A. Pagliaro,
M.S., Pharm.D., Ph.D. F.A.B.M.P., F.P.P.R., C.Psych.
Professor of Pharmacopsychology at the University of Alberta and
Associate Director of the Substance Abusology Research Unit

October 2, 2001

To you, my readers, The Bottlehopper *is not for the faint of heart. The language is street level. Much swearing, graphic descriptions and bizarre sexual encounters abound. Some may be offended. Alcoholism at the chronic stage is offensive. The disease is not pretty to observe, hear or read about. The* Bottlehopper *is brutally honest and alcoholism offends me, too. Fasten your seat belt, folks! Enjoy.*

Drunk Tank

I wake up to the stench of urine and then—when things start to focus—the almost-sweet mixture of stale vomit, stale tobacco butts, and stale bodies in their stinking clothes. A little shit in the air, too; kind of muffled. The sounds of racking tubercular coughing mixes with the snoring.

Someone tossing his guts—into the toilet, hopefully.

Welcome to the fifth-floor lock-up.

The rectangular room is poorly lit. Wire mesh surrounds the stark lightbulbs. Steel bunks are bolted to the floor along one wall. Four steel tables and benches, also bolted to the floor, run parallel to the bunks. Bars on the windows. Wouldn't be able to get by without bars. Steel and concrete are two important components of incarceration. All the rest is between your ears.

This is always the worst time in the drunk tank. When you wake up in it.

I pissed myself again.

Must have got scooped by the police. Only remember indulging in Aqua Velva. Swiped it from a drug store. Tip your head back so it doesn't stick on your tongue. Hold your breath to prevent choking. Under the high concrete next to the freeway, the damn wind felt like it wanted to kill. Train went by. Train whistles sound forlorn, melancholy. I try not to listen.

Glad I had the presence of mind to get my ass into an upper bunk. The first time, many years ago, in my innocence, I didn't know yet that the holes in the sheet-steel bunks are there for drainage purposes. I never enjoy getting urinated on. My prayer to Bacchus: *Drop me off somewhere dry, my Lord of drink.*

I've still got my instinct for the top bunk. Managed to lose everything else. All the king's horses and all the king's men. But I still haven't lost the vestiges of my self-esteem. I'm a lucky guy.

Must have mixed pills, that's it. Not Aqua Velva. Aqua Velva was that other time. Four librium and splitting a bottle of red-devil wine. I remember that much.

I wet myself, so I've been here at least three hours. That's when it lets go: after three hours. Like an alarm clock. The bladder voids. Voids. Say the secret void and win a hundred dollars.

Officer, I believe I have accidentally voided my bladder. Could I beg your kind permission to borrow a pair of dry trousers? No. I don't think that would work.

I was wrong before when I said that waking up is the worst time. When the urine cools. Perhaps this is the worst time.

No. The worst time is right after that. When you realize that you can't get a drink in this establishment. The thought hits you like a mind-control ray from outer space. Now it comes down to all the things you hate. Looking at your own reflection, for example, distorted by floating puke. Just before you flush.

I believe I am still on the record books as the youngest person ever to win the Royal Canadian Humane Society Medal for bravery. Saving a person's life. Now that's a paradox for you. A pair of ducks in my drunken stupor reasoning, my Z00Z!

The young man's sister, however, wasn't able to hold on. She drowned. When the police boats arrived to drag for her body, I learned what it means to feel inadequate. But I wouldn't come in even though there was no hope, even though it was getting dark. I had to see for myself that she was really gone. Couldn't believe that it happened. My fault?

I am by light years the most intelligent person in this drunk tank. This is what I realize every time I'm here. Then, every time, the next thought: *How fucking smart am I considering the fact I am here?*

Self-denial is a Never-Never Land.

I'm an alcoholic. Fact. It's a terrible cross to bear. Especially for me. I'll bet I'm the only person in this whole damn building who knows the chemical formula for alcohol. Phonetically, see three aitch five oh aitch.

Convoluted brain, opposable thumbs, vocal chords skillful enough to form the complexities of words. Without them, man is yet another primate. Doctor Leakey in the Olduvai Gorge. Discovering Lucy. Homo sapiens. A hundred thousand years now. Much longer I think. Jane Goodall and her chimps. Making tools. Maybe the chimps will catch up to us. Make transistor radios. Make booze.

If I'm so smart, how come I can't drink like normal people?

Got to get off this top bunk now, before the guy down there wakes up enough to feel the dampness and recognize that the loss of bladder control was not his own. Don't need a college degree to realize that liquids don't flow up. Some people have zero tolerance when it comes to getting pissed on. No sense of humor whatsoever.

Got to avoid eye contact in a place like this. Could be considered confrontational. When predators fight, there are casualties. Safer to be chameleon-like, blend with the crowd.

One resorts to physical confrontation only after expending every other means of avoidance. Then one has the moral obligation to cold-cock the aggressor, hit him as quickly and brutally as possible, so that the budding relationship won't require a second confrontation. Predators are survivors. Prey don't make it. There endeth the lesson.

Predators steal a friend's wallet, then, being kind and gentle, help him look for it. Survival requires endless hours spent foraging for money. The ability to adapt to one's environment. The true priorities: booze, food, and shelter.

I sit at the steel table benches bolted to the floor and peruse my surroundings. Wonder how they get the wire mesh between the panes of glass? Even if you got through that, steel bars on the outside of the glass will keep you a guest. Same old shit. Being a control-freak, only occasionally do I get shitfaced enough to get scooped.

Trouble is, I'm not judging my tolerance like I used to.

Normally, a pint in me and a pint on me and I can function as part of the scene. Nurse a beer or two, pass the evening away, and then in the sanctuary of the flop drink enough medicine for hopefully three or four hours of oblivion. Peace. Three hours without guilt.

Got to stop mixing pills and booze. Pretty spooky even for me. Blackouts lasting six to ten hours. My father would turn over in his grave if he knew. Dad left us in 1969, the year my son and heir was born. Now, I think, it's 1975. Yeah it is. This was not my goal in life—drinking vanilla, rubbing alcohol, squeeze (Sterno or Canned Heat), Lysol, as the norm. The drug-store elixirs exacerbating the progression into petit and grand mal seizures during withdrawal, getting recognized as a repeat customer in Vancouver's emergency rooms, malnutrition, wine sores that don't heal because of the debilitated lymphatic system. Blood that won't coagulate; no platelets.

My blood's still red, though. I truly am a lucky guy.

Close your eyes and wish you were back in Kansas. It doesn't work, though. As Oliver Hardy would say to Stan Laurel, it's a fine mess you've gotten us into. The ridiculous bowler hat on his chubby head. Pudgy fingers nervously manipulating his tie. Laurel and Hardy, comic geniuses.

Some fucking idiot is making a scene. Stupid place to have the belt-buckle-cowboy-hat gene that drives you to pick a fight. Tiny, a cop, loves these challenges to his authority.

Tiny once killed a guy with his hands, as the story goes, and he enjoys keeping the peace in the lock-up now. Because of his size and his propensity to handle disclipine physically, he is no longer allowed on the street. I have learned about Tiny by observation. Assume a submissive posture before the alpha male. Like wolves. On the dominant person's turf: he thinks shit and you slide. Survival skills, hard-learned survival skills.

The asshole is still performing. It won't be long now before Tiny removes him to a far worse place.

I remember the two pot-heads who once lit a joint in the fifth-floor lock-up. I hit the upper bunk—a refuge from the downstream benefits—and feigned sleep. Even so I took a nightstick to the kidneys twice before Tiny eliminated me as too drunk to be a suspect in the smoke-in.

I don't think the longhairs had any idea how much damage can be done with a knotted wet towel applied to the kidneys and other parts of the anatomy. Rolled-up telephone books accomplish the same level of pain without breaking skin. So you piss a little blood; that doesn't hurt. The blunt-force trauma and deep bruising is what hurts. I have yet to be on the receiving end of this systematic touch therapy, but I have observed the results.

The longhairs were brain-dead to light the fucking joint in the first place. The cops think shit, I slide. Therefore I am. Therefore I survive. Simple.

The attitude change after a beating. Sort of a tune-up from the neck up. Not much visible in the way of trauma; just a lot of pain and bruising, hardly ever any blood. If there were, it could be explained away as the use of reasonable force to subdue the drunk in the initial arrest. Ever view the Rodney King tape of reasonable force? I rest my case.

No one ever believes a drunk.

Good god. Only fifteen minutes have gone by. Will six hours ever pass?

What the fuck. You do the crime, you do the time. Tiny has removed the troublemaker; we won't see him again. Perhaps I can put my head down and get some rest. Mercifully, the time sometimes passes more quickly when my eyes are closed. Problem is, I can't close my mind. Unable to control the thought process.

Shit! Some asshole's having a seizure. Must have got scooped when he was in withdrawal. That's why they only keep us here six hours. Can't have the whole darn place going into withdrawal. Too inconvenient. The grand mal seizure voids both bladders and all six miles of bowels. Mercifully, no recollection. Try to stop him from hurting himself. Keep your fingers out of harm's way. You learn to say this: fuck him, let him flop.

Been there done that. He's fucking up my karma! You get all kinds in here—cry-babies, tough guys. So if you do the crime, you do the time; don't expect any sympathy from me, asshole.

Fee,fi,fo,fum. A fart slips from my bum. The down side of drinking vanilla: when you flatulate, you smell like a sick Christmas cake. If it's a damp one, and it frequently is, it can really confuse the olfactory system. Pack the anus with tissue. Damage control. For clean pants, go to the Sally Anne. Smelling like that. Leave a Christmas cake in the changing room. Wear your clean slacks and disappear into the sunset. Who was that quiet, vanilla-smelling man? High-ho, Stinko, away! All he left were the pants.

Bob's my name. Booze is my game.

No one notices when I spell my name backwards.

Iambic pentameter has no parameters. Does one have to wear a bonnet to write a good sonnet? Walter Raleigh lost his head when Kew Eee One wanted him dead. Stone walls do not a prison make, nor iron bars a cage. In a cage, in a rage, born free, as free as the vanilla wind blows.

Seventeen more minutes have passed.

According to consensus, the line between sanity and insanity is finite. Therefore I am somewhere on the Yellow Brick Road to Emerald City or in a flash like jumping jack flash or it could be that we all live in a Yellow Submarine, a Yellow Submarine. Whomever said, and it was I, once, that "the acquisition of knowledge nourishes the intellect and enriches the soul" was bullshitting. If anyone needs medicine, it's me. I hate it when I'm zooming like this, zooming. I call it the Zooz—cooking, out of control. Zooz is a palindrome, just like me. When the rabbit howls. Jupiter isn't aligned with Mars. Have to get numb to escape this fun. Hark, what light through yonder bars breaks?

It is the sun.

The metallic clang of the keeper's gate. "You fucking assholes, get the fuck out of here." The sweetest words.

The glass is definitely half full.

We go forth to face the challenges of the new day, complete with our mission statement, getting on the critical path, setting goals—good little bottlehoppers shuffling out of the tank. Want to take a walk on the wild side? Want to Do the Dew? Follow me. Big wheels keep on turning, proud drunk keeps on burning. Rolling. Rolling. Rolling through life my way.

I step into the greasy twilight of dawn, and the wind out of a dead alley smacks me like a wet towel. I wasn't always like this. I'm a casualty of Ethyl, Ethyl Alcohol, the "witchy bitch." My mistress Ethyl won me, and now owns my soul.

Go for the Gusto

We shall leave the disgusting shadow of the man we met in our first chapter. There will be plenty of time later to examine his sojourn on Skid Road, check in with his new lifestyle, and follow some of his more bizarre escapades.

After all, boB has five more years to go before he starts climbing slowly out of the quicksand of his doomed love affair with Ethyl, and sometimes Methyl, alcohol. We will have no problem finding him; I will always know where he is. He is me.

Please do not confuse empathy with sympathy for boB. Neither Bob nor boB nor the Bottlehopper want sympathy. Yogi Berra said, "When you reach the fork in the road—take it." We did just that.

It's impossible to rationalize with the chemically dependent. After the choice is made to live on the treadmill of chronic alcohol addiction, few make it back to tell the story.

However, there was a before—before alcoholism, before boB, and before the Bottlehopper. So, drawing on the inspiration of that wonderful book Young Winston, I'm focusing this chapter on the life of Young Bob. Of course, it's presumptuous of me even to mention Winston Churchill, that distinguished and dynamic product of the twentieth century, in the context of my insignificant life. Churchill led a cavalry charge in the Sudan against the Mahadi, got captured and escaped twice in the Boer War, served as First Lord of the Admiralty, then as Prime Minister of Great Britain. He just about lived long enough to see humans walk on the moon. But if there is something to be gleaned from my formative years, let us go a-forth (or a-fifth of cheap whiskey) and explore it, or me, the shadow, the shadow before the darkness, when the sun was still at noon or higher—the shadow's childhood, my education, my first marriage, and the beginning of my squalid affair.

Picture me as a predator, as a young tyrannosaurus rex, charging ruthlessly through life and devouring every morsel. Bob goes forth like a thunder lizard, lurching compulsively and obsessively towards his own Big Bang that will herald the end of his personal Cretaceous period. The hell of chemical dependency—the period of boB, in which the man takes a drink, the drink takes a drink, and then the drink takes the man—still lurks ominously in the future. By some miracle, the man will survive and his resurrection, called the Bottlehopper, will emerge, nurtured on the seas of alcohol, washed by waves of anger. These huge waves smash against the shore in towering sets of guilt, remorse, fear, and self-loathing...

Born in Scotland in nineteen forty-three, at the age of four Bottlehopper emigrates with his family to Canada. The nuclear family places him as the third of four children. Nothing unusual about that. It is interesting to note, however, that his older sister and brother are his seniors by thirteen and eleven years respectively. Hardly an excuse for chemical dependency, but there are times when any excuse will do.

Bob is conceived late in his parents' life, an admitted surprise. His younger sister is even less valid—an afterthought. The Bottlehopper's parents often joke good-naturedly about the surprise factor. In reality, the two younger children, growing up in their parents' chosen new country, give the Edwards elders much joy and pride. They certainly keep Mom and Dad young.

Bob's older sister marries a partner for life. Ordinarily we would consider her good example to be a stroke of luck for the young man. But Christiene has passed out of her own childhood so long before Bob enters his formative years that she seems to him little more than a fading ghost at the end of a dark hallway, an aunt, an unremembered face in the family photo album.

Older brother Billy is bisexual long before the practice gains a certain social respectability. Billy's choice of an AC/DC lifestyle drives a wedge between the sons; so does the difference in years and the lack of common interests—except for swimming. Perhaps a good analogy would be Raging Bull meets Greg Louganis. The older brother's sexual preferences might have been influenced by Mom's strong personality. No matter. Billy is the antipode—too good-looking, sensitive, articulate, artistic. Wouldn't say shit even if he had a mouthful.

The younger sibling sensitive and female worships the Bottlehopper as a role model. Today, over twenty years later, she is still unable to cope with the trauma and reality of his alcoholism. Sadly for Margaret, she chooses not to forgive her brother Bob.

The Bottlehopper becomes the "golden boy" of the family. A natural athlete with blond curly hair and blue eyes, he uses his looks and his gift for the vernacular to win many a young lady's heart. Relentlessly Bob pursues his ultimate goal of getting in their panties. He learns early in the game not to kiss and tell. Keeping his lip zipped increases his popularity with the opposite sex. Thus he discovers a principle of marketing that will one day earn him a lot of money—that word-of-mouth is the best form of advertising.

Thanks for the memories, girls.

Bottlehopper's younger sister is much like the sensitive older brother—easily hurt. Mother pushes their buttons. The Edwards matriarch is a strong lady; she can annihilate a personality, literally devour and dominate. Young Bob learns a trick or two from her and dominates the weaker personalities of the older and younger siblings. He is the most like mother in looks and personality. Two blue-eyed hellions are they.

My Orange Protestant father is a man's man. A Scottish Archie Bunker. "We won the bloody battle of the Boyne, didn't we?" He has an exceptional sense of humor, worships his wife, and puts up with her domineering ways. But only to a point.

The shadow also learns how to handle mother—by manipulation, confrontation, and resistance. Ultimately he establishes equality in their codependent behavior.

The pre-school years are idyllic. The family home is a gingerbread two-story, bought after only two months in Canada. The setting lies in the "Royal City"—New Westminster, British Columbia. The handsome old home sits kitty-corner to a large public park. Moody Park is a paradise of softball diamonds, diving boards, tennis courts, lacrosse boxes, soccer pitches, and open spaces to fly kites. The family home sits on two lots, plenty of elbow room. Four magnificent trees provided an annual abundance of cherries, apples, and pears. Hordes of kids provide a cast of characters that would have satisfied Dickens. Always a pick-up game of the sport in season. One potato, two potato, three potato, four. Second captain, first pick. The pungent aroma of linseed oil on a black-diamond glove. Crisp fall days and the crunch of young bodies playing tackle. The unforgettable smell of grass stains. Steamy summer days spent swimming for five hours in the Kinsman Pool. At day's end, freighted with food, he slips into an exhausted sleep, a sleep so intense that Rapid Eye Movement moves in slow motion. Then the young lion wakes, fully refreshed, batteries charged, and fills the bottomless pit with more fuel, then surges forward into the day's activities. This remains Bob's family's home until long after he jumps into the nuptial bed.

The junior and senior high years are *like American Graffiti.* Sports, chicks, cars, chicks, homework, chicks, vacations, chicks, drinking, chicks...The secret trysts are still a secret with Bob. He never burns any bridges sexually, and this enables him to go back for second helpings in lean times. Words don't exist in his vocabulary to adequately describe the joy of growing up.

What a HOOT! Perhaps that conveys it.

My childhood cannot be blamed for my alcoholism. I wasn't abused physically, sexually, or mentally. At every point, Bob knows where he's going. He just doesn't know how devastating the trip will be.

Alcohol is an enormous part of these years. At this stage, it's "God's gift that gladdens the heart." Later, Bob will decide that God has a wicked sense of humor. For example, God picked the Jews to be his "chosen people." The pogroms in Russia, the Holocaust, the Middle East today... Sure glad the Scots weren't chosen. But who fucking cares about the philosophies of a disgusting skid-row derelict?

I reply quietly and sincerely: "People will pay to hear me speak—because there is an after."

After much struggle, after many brushes with death, there is an after. Happiness beyond even my wildest dreams. That's what this book is about. Go for the gusto, grab the ring, take control of the rudder that steers your life. Look fifteen years younger inside, where it counts.

Plain Robert Edwards is my given name. Other than the lack of a middle name, nothing much in my upbringing indicates any propensity towards alcoholism. But I'll let you decide that.

Bob matured very young, both physically and sexually. The jury is still out on the mental maturity. Even today, at age fifty-five.

The year 1958 found me in grade nine. British Columbia was celebrating its hundred-year anniversary of joining the Confederation of Canada. The cool thing was to grow a beard, or huge mutton-chop sideburns. I was pretty cool, even at fourteen years old. A lot of sophomores couldn't grow one. Even some of the seniors. Macho Bob, jock extraordinaire. Face it, Bob—in your eyes, you were Mr. Studly.

The mystery of the differences in reproductive organs. How they fit together. Breasts. This sex business consumed much of my focus. The excitement of discovery and experimentation. I was an apt student of this discipline.

Truth is, I never got to the promised land very often. Hell, if a girl became pregnant you either married her or they took you out of town, put you in a hole, and threw rocks at you. This was the Age Of The Holy Hymen. The girls were terrified; me, too.

Being a gamer, I tried. My status symbol was the ring embossed in the leather of my wallet—created by the rubber I used to carry just in case I got lucky. Hell, lions only make a kill—what is it?—once in ten attempts? Persistence brings success.

Even in those years I was focused, setting goals, staying on my critical path. I had my mandate in life. Of course, I never knew any of these terms in those years. All Bob wanted was to get laid well, and often. And even if not well, often.

I was formidable—just over five foot ten inches and a rock-solid one eighty-five pounds. I had pubic hair in grade seven. I was a raging hormone! As a native North American once said, "Me know how. Don't know who." The key was to find someone, "*anyone*", female to "how" with.

Sports and cold showers dominated my life. Each season brought a new sport. I loved them all; I excelled at them all. Every year, three letters. Actually, it was four in junior high. I played organized baseball until age twenty. Played junior football and junior lacrosse until twenty-one, and I swam competitively. After graduation, I kept playing lacrosse. My junior-league team was finalist in three Minto-Cup championships, and my senior-league team, Labatt's Blues, won the national championship. I attended the rookie development camps for the B.C. Lions football team. I loved the challenge, the winning, and the camaraderie. Hell, I even learned to lose somewhat graciously.

My physical size and strength allowed me to secure a job in the lumber mill. I started working just a month or so before my fifteenth birthday. I was too young, legally. But my dad was personnel manager, so I scored a job that paid big bucks—one dollar sixty-five cents an hour. My god, over thirteen dollars a day! I was a man of means—a card-carrying member of the IWA.

The IWA is the last and only union I ever joined. Instead I became one of the vanishing breed of true capitalists. Even in those pubescent years I felt the unions had already accomplished their original mandate—which was to take care of their members, to create safer workplaces, and to gain compensation for work-related injuries. They had already established the idea of hiring on the basis of seniority, of limiting the work week to forty hours, of providing extra pay for holidays and overtime. Even then I felt that a strike is a dumb way to settle any issue, including a dispute about money. Hell, especially money.

Employees on strike are unhappy people. After one day on strike, they've made their point. But the strike can keep going for another two thousand days. I'm not a member of Mensa, but it seems obvious to me that strikes are lose-lose situations. Union workers may win a few concessions, but they never earn enough to pay back their losses. The companies lose big-time as well, and so does the entire economy of the country. Why not settle disputes with compulsory, impartial third-party arbitration? Then if the union refuses to go back to work, the company can hire new employees. If the company refuses to accept the terms of the settlement, the government can punish them with fines.

Enough of this sense!

Having a union job helped me grow up fast. On my fifteenth birthday we were getting ready for the annual government safety inspections at the lumber mill. I worked the day shift in the power house, cleaning the inside of a boiler. We were standing in the combustion chamber chipping klinker—melted bricks—off the grates. Hot, dirty, and hard work.

My co-workers knew it was my birthday. While we chipped and sweated, they made plans to celebrate. They wanted to take me to the bar after work. My orders were to keep my hard-hat on, keep the dirt on my face, keep my back to the bar, and keep my mouth shut. The legal age for drinking was twenty-one, so I had some realistic fears about bringing this off. But as they say, God hates a coward!

And in fact I actually got served.

Just wait until my friends hear about this, I kept thinking. *I'm becoming a man of the world.*

I only remember drinking the first six or so twelve-ounce glasses of beer. They went down like nectar of the gods. Then I remember people hustling me to a car... me tossing my guts in a parking lot for the first time... being left on my front verandah at home. The verandah turning into a space ship doing warp speed through a vomiting universe of puke. At first I thought I would die. Then I wished I would. When I closed my eyes, I was riding a tilt-a-whirl gone bloody berserk. When I opened my eyes, I puked. I believe I actually vomited myself sober. My hands were sore the next day from the death-grip I had on the verandah.

The devil takes care of his own. Mom and Dad had gone out for the evening, so I actually got away with this adventure. How I negotiated the stairs is a mystery. Didn't dare try to take a shower—I probably would have drowned. But I wiped myself clean with a wet cloth and gargled and brushed my teeth. My mouth tasted vile with bile. Amazingly, I even managed to throw my vomit-covered clothes in the washing machine and fire it up. By the time my parents got home, I was fast asleep in bed.

Because my parents never found out, I gained respect with my co-workers. I was a man who could be trusted. I was also sitting tall in the saddle with my peers. My first drinking bout had elevated my stature. I liked that.

I suppose my career in the lumber mill could have gone one of two ways. Because of my father's position in the company, I could have taken the job easy—put my time in and made love to the dog—for a while, at least. I chose to go the other way and be a real over-achiever. I enjoyed working, and I was fun to work with. Plus, they were paying me money. Have fun; make money—I liked that. Money opened doors. Money improved my standard of living. I could spend money on chicks.

Word of my work ethic got around, and many of the department heads wanted me to work for them. As a result, I learned to do many different jobs. I covered for steady employees at Christmas, Easter, and in the summer. Weekends, too.

Thanks to the work ethic, I was only a high-school junior when I bought my first car—a nineteen fifty-one Chevy. If you can imagine, the price of gas was thirty cents a gallon. The bloody car itself only cost three hundred dollars. That was a decent price for a quick education in car-ownership mistakes. For example, I thought the headliner (the interior ceiling) would look cool if I painted it white. So I did that, and it did look cool—at first. Overnight, though, as the paint dried, the headliner shrunk. The next morning I had a ridiculous half-inch gap around the entire interior of the roof. This attempt at customizing cost me fifty dollars to repair.

The best feature in the car was its front seat, which was broken. I had a board jammed in to hold it in the proper place. When

I went to the "finger bowl" (the drive-in) with my squeeze-of-the-month, all I needed to do was remove the board and, like magic, create acres of horizontal space.

While attending junior college I met my first wife. Like me, she was a free spirit; she was majoring in Cafeteria 100, Class-Skipping 101, and Chips-and-Gravy 102. Her dad had won the Governor General's Medal for scholastic achievement. I knew when he found out about her attitude, the labor force would be growing by one young lady. It was only a matter of time.

Her dad was a research chemist at the University of British Columbia, and is truly a remarkable man. He's a member of Mensa, but he can spit and chaw with the best of them—a rare quality among the elite in intelligence. He also possesses manual skills; he understands cars better than most mechanics. If he wants to know something, he learns it. For example, he wanted to speak Japanese when they went to the Olympic games in Osaka (I believe the year was 1964). This remarkable man took several courses to learn Japanese. Then he spent time hanging around Japanese funerals so he could hear and practice the language. I love this guy!

My mother-in-law is one of the kindest, most thoughtful people in this world. She is a little like Edith Bunker from the old *All in the Family* television show. In this unique case the comparison is a compliment.

These two wonderful human beings, formerly my in-laws, found it in their hearts to forgive me when I turned up back on the coast in 1981. I was the guy who had deserted their oldest child and abandoned their grandchild, my only son, for ten bloody years. By then I'd started a new life. But they remembered how I'd been before I got sick. They took me into their home and were delighted that I was alive and well. They actually forgave me, and more. My mother-in-law even eased the pain and guilt I felt for not being there when my own mother died.

"Bob," she said, "of the four children in your family, you spent more time and took more care of your ailing parents than the three others combined. Then you got sick. Be thankful that you're well, and your mother will be happy. We are."

Thanks, to both my in-laws, from my heart.

Our wedding was on July 6,1966. By then I was very successful in real estate, and because of this we were able to go to Hawaii for our three-week honeymoon. We stayed up by Fort De Russey, right on Waikiki Beach. Gosh, there were even some grass shacks on the beach in those days. The Vietnam War was in full swing, and there were plenty of young men in uniforms. The Ala Moana Shopping Center was just being built with parking for an amazing ten thousand cars. That scale of things boggled my mind.

These were good years, my early married life. I lived with gusto.

For example, we spent almost a month at Montreal's Expo 67 in la belle province of Quebec. To get a feeling for the size of Canada, we took the train. Never again, for me. It took us three days and nights just to get to Ottawa, which is only about sixty-five percent of the way to the Atlantic Ocean. It's actually closer to go from Vancouver to Hawaii than it is from Vancouver to Montreal.

As we rolled through miles of bald-headed prairies, rock, and the bare limbs of stunted deciduous trees, I started to go stir-crazy. My salvation was the bar car. When we crossed from one province into another, the crew had to remove our unfinished drinks and replace them with fresh ones. I tried to have at least two drinks pretty well gone as we approached the next province. Then I would get two full ones.

I suppose it was part of my Scottish heritage, being a "haggis eating oatmeal savage" and all.

But I can't blame my Gaelic genes for turning me into an alcoholic. In fact, I could take forever rummaging around in the closet of my past and still fail to produce the precise cause-and-effect for my problem with alcohol. If my search was earnest, though, I would spend a good part of that time rummaging through the year 1969.

This was the pivotal year in my life. My dad died July 24, 1969. My only son and heir was born August twenty-fourth—one month later to the day. The delivery was incredibly difficult; it finally ended in a Caesarian. But that wasn't the end. My wife's health problems continued after she came home with the baby. One night she broke into tears and told me that she was having trouble seeing. She didn't feel that she could safely drive a car. Approximately one month after that, she was legally blind.

Tumor? Cancer? What in God's name was it? I was frantic! Suddenly life consisted of appointments with a hoard of doctors and specialists. If we hung around many more X-ray machines, we were all going to start glowing in the night. That was my little joke in those days. Whistling in the dark.

How tough it was to watch someone I loved getting progressively more ill. I was powerless to help. It was the first thing in my candy-ass life that I couldn't handle. I felt guilt, frustration.

Several months passed before we had a name for her illness. Multiple sclerosis. She grew a mustache from the side-effects of

Prednisone, a steroid used to treat the disease. She retained fluid and swelled up. They call that the "moon-face reaction."

By then I was already drinking with a purpose.

1969 marked the end of my intelligent life. I drank to control my fears. I became a loner. Sexual trysts were noncomittal; superficial bar conversations sufficed. Quite simply, I could not cope.

The collapse didn't happen overnight. Alcoholism is progressive. Later, I would learn the psychology of the disease. For now, I was learning the mathematics—if one is good, a double is twice as good. And the square root of four is two. I was a goner!

I am being as honest about this as I know how. No one gets any blame, and I don't want your sympathy. Bob chose the path he took. I certainly didn't know where it was going to lead me. But I did know that when I was numb with booze I didn't hurt.

I must have believed that I could degrade myself and punish myself for however long I deemed necessary and then I could just pick up the remnants of my life and start over. As we shall see, getting back on my feet was going to be no easy task.

The Alcoholic Personality

We are going to investigate my "alcoholic personality."

To understand myself— my strengths and weaknesses, how I deal with feelings, how I respond to daily challenges both small and big—this is an ongoing process. The academic would, perhaps, identify my character defects, my co-dependent behavior, my self-centered tendencies, and wonder whether or not I believed her when my mother caught me yanking on my "special purpose" and then informed me that such activity would result in my going blind. (I'd like to say that I only continued until I needed glasses. Truth is, my prescription kept getting stronger and stronger.)

I am a remarkable piece of work! In my opinion, my character exhibits many strengths and weaknesses, and let me offer one example of both—I have a compulsive-obsessive behavior disorder.

That's a kinder, gentler way of saying that I'm close to being manic-depressive. You know—a balanced personality half-manic, half-depressive. But what the fuck. We all have our crosses to bear.

Perhaps I'll begin with some of my heroes. Vince Lombardi, Green Bay's hall-of-fame football coach, has my admiration as a sports icon. His philosophy was this: One plays hurt, but never let the bastard know he hurt you. Compliment the opponent by saying (if you can speak) that your mother could hit harder, and did. Tell the opposition, by using the media, that you're going to pull your guards (Cramer and Thurston) to lead the sweep off-tackle. Forrest Gregg, your all-pro-offensive tackle, is going to neutralize their defensive end. Jim Taylor, the fullback, will lead block for Paul Horning. WE ARE GOING TO RAM IT DOWN YOUR THROAT. You tell them what you're going to do, and then you do it! That's fucking awesome! Not only could I play hurt for a coach like this, I would look forward to it. I would excel at it.

I have observed this many times on the tube—Lombardi's middle linebacker and the others on defense pairing off and giving each other forearm shivers to the head. Touch therapy to get into the desired mind-set before going out on the field. Can you imagine how the other team feels?

General George S. Patton said, "The most exhilarating condition the human spirit can achieve is war." He's another guy who had huge balls. A brilliant general and tactician, Patton was a proponent of the lead-by-example doctrine. "Shell shock" did not program in his thought-process. During the Italian campaign he punched a traumatized American soldier in the head. He just couldn't believe that the man wasn't having as much fun killing Germans as he was. Consensus puts Rommel and Patton as two of the best fighting generals of World War II.

Patton may have been a little flaky, with the reincarnated Roman warrior stuff, but he could well have played for another of my favorites, Julius Caesar. Veni, vidi, vici— I really admire this attitude. And Caesar had the "falling sickness." Me, too. I drank, I got drunk, I fell down. I also admired his ego, fooling around with a crumpet like Cleopatra. When asked if the age difference would cause sexual problems, he said, "If she dies, she dies. I love having sex." You gotta love the attitude.

Actually I made up that sex part. But ask yourself—could you see him saying it? Damned right!

Alexander the Great took care of the Gordian Knot. Local legend said that whoever could untie the knot would conquer Asia Minor. Alexander scoped out the knot, called a time out, retired to his tent to strategize, came back in front of his army, waited until the right moment, pulled his sword and CUT the knot. I'd have followed him anywhere. Wouldn't you?

I forgot something else about Caesar. Listening skills and the "Ides of March." His choice of friends and "Et tu, Brute." Could these be classed as character defects? Balancing the yin and the yang. Heck, Oedipus "really loved" his mom. Did he respect her in the morning?

Brian Kelly, an all-Canadian receiver for the Edmonton Eskimos, when asked why he didn't spike the ball, do the hula, or break into a can-can dance after scoring a touchdown, humbly replied, "I try to act as though I've been in the end zone before." Kelly has owned the Canadian Football record for most touchdowns in a season for over ten years.

The more I chose to swim in the liquidarium called alcoholism, the more mysterious it became and the less I laughed. If boB could speak, he would warn you to remember to laugh at yourself and at other funny things in your life. This laughing at life is an acquired defensive mechanism of survival. But I lost my sense of humor under the burden of all-consuming guilt and paralyzing fear. Every time I lost self-esteem, I moved on to the next stage of my journey.

I actually thought at first that this alcoholism gig was a type of a game. Snakes and ladders, Monopoly, that sort of thing. "What a maroon," as Bugs Bunny would say. The "I-can-fix-it" Bob, the "I-can-win Bob", the "I-can-learn-how" Bob disappeared from the frontal lobe. The contrary boB became dominant. In the rare moments when Bob was around and trying to stop the insanity, he could never get past a profound discovery—in the liquidarium, there is no "off" switch.

The terrifying realization that I couldn't stop triggered an avalanche of suicidal thoughts. Irrational behavior became normal; fear was my constant companion; depression, anger, and futility were daily events. The only time I was at peace occurred when I was numb with drink or unconscious. "Yabba dabba do," to quote another hero, Fred Flintstone. Pepe le Pew the horny skunk, the Tasmanian Devil, Yosemite Sam, and Foghorn Leghorn the bullshitting rooster—all my heroes!

Can a problem develop if I look too deeply into the inner self? Perhaps I'll find out more than I can handle. But my attitude—lead, I'll follow. Talk, I'll listen. Better yet, don't just stand there get the hell out of my way. Definitely an overachiever's mind set.

I am a Bold-Amiable personality type. Had you guessed? Absolutely no analytical skills exist in my personality. For example, if

I'm putting something together, the first thing I do is throw away the instructions. There are always parts left over, and the thing never works right. My wife Pat retrieves the instructions and, if you can imagine, actually peruses them. Then she gets all the right tools, lays everything out, and voila! The problem is solved. I love her because of—and in spite of—this skill. But if you want a touchdown inside the ten-yard line, where the price of real estate goes up, give me the ball! If there is only one match left, I'll light the cigarette. The early Bob used to thrive on pressure, rise to the occasion. I'm a fucking Looney Tune, just like my role models.

Had you guessed?

I'm not big on delayed gratification, either. I have no mountains left to climb. But there are a few hills remaining. I broke a tooth boogie-boarding last year on Maui. This year, I broke my collarbone—playing volleyball, no less. God, I love the rush. Being on the edge. The adrenaline buzz! Jumped off a couple of new waterfalls this year; good forty-footers. ZOOZ!

These adventures are not acting out a death wish; it's more a celebration of life. And believe me, after all I've been through, I'm beginning to learn where to draw the line. Last year my major goal was to pay real money to jump out of a perfectly good airplane. Sky-diving, what a hoot that would be—especially for a guy who doesn't like to climb ladders. But the doctor said, "No way. Not in this life." Now that I'm wiser, I choose to obey him.

AA requires rigorous honesty in all your affairs—honesty as if your life depended on it. In fact, my life *does* depend on it. If I start bullshitting myself again, I'm gone.

Answer this one, then, oh omniscient one: Why do they have flotation gear under your seat on an aircraft? Especially over land flights. A fucking parachute would make an infinitely more suitable piece of equipment to this rum-soaked, wine-dipped, vanilla-cured dude.

Let's Dew It! More caffeine for you in it. Fact is, almost double other beverages. Gargle with Scope first, but don't spit it out. That elixir runs about eighteen percent alcohol on a hydrometer. All right, men, we're going over the top. Everyone gargle and swallow three times. CHARGE!

Did I mention a sense of humor? More a sense of the bizarre, perhaps. With me there are no surprises; what you see is what you get. I have learned to speak with a straight tongue.

I got a tattoo on Maui this year. If you think I was being macho, guess again. After all, I live with three dominant women and a neutered female cat. They lower their standards and treat me as an equal. Gran says I'm the boss when no one's at home. I think that means the cat, too.

Women who compete with men in any endeavor lack ambition. Why? Because to compete with men they have to lower their standards.

Sometimes I have the thought that God is female.

The tattoo is around my left bicep, a simple Hawaiian design representing "tapa" cloth. Above it are two crossed "kapu" sticks. The sticks mean "keep out" in Hawaiian lore. Symbolically: No More Shit In This Body. I even left a tiny gap in the circle; this will allow my spirit or "mana" to leave when I die. Could this be construed as Bob trying to cover all the bases as he grows older?

The feeling of getting tattooed, by the way—for you men out there—is similar to getting your weenie caught in your zipper. Especially on the underside of your bicep. Why, then, get the underside done? It's sort of like kissing your sister if you don't.

I'm off-the-wall, I admit it. For example, how about a personal fantasy? If there is such a thing as reincarnation, I hope to come back as a really great racehorse, a stallion, and win the Triple Crown. That's like batting four hundred, and no one's done that since Ted Williams. Then the good part: I'd pull up a little lame. Nothing serious; say, shin splints. Now comes the best part. I'm syndicated for millions, set up with all the Kentucky bluegrass I can eat and all the fillies I can handle. Don't wake me now!

Northern Dancer, to my shame as a Canadian, got this set-up. Hard to believe. He was indifferent at first. Instead of iron shoes, he was wearing loafers with tassels. Fortunately, it was a combination of being shy and not knowing what to do. They showed him some blue horse movies.

That's a true story. Somewhat embellished, but that's okay. It makes for better telling.

In the business world I was a big success. Sales and marketing, where else? I led by example—a can-do sort of guy, a super employee, goal-oriented, success-driven. An idea man. More than that, I followed through on the idea and made things happen. A workaholic. I would have hired a clone of myself, only if he were sober.

I was a take-charge leader. Got paid tons of money. Strong, inspirational, an over-achiever. Able to bring out the strengths of our employees. Firmly believed in stretching the envelope. Get yourself out of comfort zones. One of the last of the vanishing breed of capitalists. Truly the type of guy who loved the hunt and lived the chase. It's great fun to be in my jet-stream.

I find that hard work is the common denominator. Even if your product is good, your sales skills equal, and your price the same, I still kick ass because I'll outwork you. I was brought up right. I have strong values, say please and thank you, and never had the balls to be a crook. Never got a drunk-driving charge. That doesn't mean I didn't drive drunk; it does mean that I was lucky, and that I took a lot of cabs. Never hit my wife nor any other woman. Such cowardice goes against everything I believe in.

Challenges and fears—how we choose to deal with them determines if we grow. Growth is power! Knowledge is power! I was like a giant mutating member of the phylum Porifera—the sponge. I soaked up knowledge.

How can anyone appear so Cool Hand Luke outside and yet be so vulnerable inside? That's a paradox, "a pair of ducks" in boB's land of Zooz.

Certainly I am entrepreneurial in my thinking. I continue to water the seeds of my investments because the seeds of greatness aren't in you if you can't save some. I made a lot of employers wealthy and, almost as a by-product of my success, became more than financially secure.

The alcoholic personality may be off the wall, but that wild energy can be turned into an asset. If you can take the focus required to forage for alcohol and re-channel it into your vocation, the power of prescription dictates that this total commitment and focus will result in wealth. As a result of your natural work ethic, you find wealth almost by serendipity. If you confidently expect to succeed, you will. What the mind can conceive, the man can achieve.

"This is your life!" Remember the old TV show? Actually, it's my life.

Enterprise this is Captain Kirk. Beam this boB guy up, Mr. Scott, and warn Spock not to try a Vulcan Mind Lock. This humanoid is dangerous! Just tell Dr. McCoy his liver is already pickled. The brain stem has been frozen once, using an external energy force called Fudge Sicles." Just tell Dr. McCoy to sedate the rest for future study. *Be sure to keep him in restraint. Mr. Scott, keep him away from any grain or methyl alcohol. This specimen is pretty well stunned, so you can lower the power settings on your phasers.*

The reference to a frozen brain involves boB, some really good weed called Thai sticks, Monday-night football, fifteen or so Fudge Sicles, and the raving "munchies." The result: I almost got hypothermia. That night, Howard Cosell made sense (sort of... just this one time...). Enough said!

The specific details of the adventure are left to the reader's imagination.

Birch Bay Hero

The year is 1954. I am eleven years old, almost twelve. The setting is the Pacific Northwest just outside Blaine, Washington—Birch Bay.

For at least sixteen of my growing-up years my family crossed the border from British Columbia every summer to vacation at the Bay. In fact, I continue to visit Birch Bay; last summer, my wife Pat and I spent two nights at the state park in a rented Volkswagen van. (Pat doesn't "do tents.")

The Bay resonates with so many wonderful memories of my late parents, my family, and my friends. The state park is a super place—lots of trees with large camping spots and plenty of fire pits. God! I love that place. I spent my most memorable growing-up summers there bike-riding, horseback-riding, swimming, water-skiing, crabbing, clamming, gathering oysters, rollerskating—just about every activity a boy growing up can imagine.

Of course, trauma is memorable, too.

I want to tell you about a beautiful summer day. My dad, my younger sister Margaret, and I were doing something we really enjoyed—crabbing as the tide went out. Lots of sun and a light breeze off the ocean. Great stuff!

The idea of crabbing was to follow the tide out, wearing sneakers and carrying burlap sacks, to search the seaweed in knee-deep water for that most succulent of all shellfish, the dungeness crab. We used my old lacrosse sticks to pick them up because these crustaceans have pinchers that can break the skin. Ouch!

(Actually, crabbing wouldn't have been so much fun without the danger. Suddenly I realize that the being-on-the-edge component of my personality was fully operative at eleven years old.)

We carefully checked each crab for the critical measurement, at least six and one-fourth inches across the shell. Dad was a real stickler for this regulation. He explained that if immature crabs were taken, even by just a little, there wouldn't be any left in a few years.

We almost always got our limit of eight each. If the truth were known, that's the main reason we took Margaret—for her limit in crabs. She really wasn't into crabbing, but she got to spend time with two really important guys in her life, Dad and me. We paid special attention to her. This was my first symbiotic experience in interpersonal relationships. I was growing up, developing manipulative skills already. Great stuff! Great times!

The merchants at Birch Bay had decided to dispense vouchers for free gifts by putting them inside balloons and then dropping the balloons out of an airplane. I remember watching the balloons containing the goodies as they wafted down out of the sky: free cases of RC Cola (a favorite beverage), Coke, Pepsi, free tickets to the roller skating rink, rides at the amusement park. Innocuous enough.

But there was a problem. When the tide goes out, so does the wind. Any balloons not captured by eager young hands bounced out to the ocean and stuck there, caught by the exposed seaweed of the low tide.

Kids and water!

The hell of it was this: Directly under the balloons there was deep water, sort of a drop-off or channel. The kids could walk out on the sandbars toward the balloons, near the balloons, but to actually get the prizes they had to scoot themselves out into "can't-touch-the-bottom depth." They had to go just beyond their range, where the sinister seaweed strands were waiting to wrap around their ankles and seem to be pulling, like claws from below in the worst nightmare of your life. That alone could scare you to death.

This was going to be a lethal trap. While we weren't looking, two kids from Washington, a boy and girl about my age, got into trouble big trouble right in front of us.

The first thing that interrupted my crabbing was noise. Noise that wasn't right. Noise that broke the spell. Noise with that inference in tone and syntax – "that I'm-in-trouble" sound. The air was filled with the "grab-you-by-the-balls" sounds of terror—the sounds that only children with a lifetime to live can make, the sounds a drowning man makes when he reaches for a straw. Terror resonates with a tone of its own.

Dad noticed about the same time as me. "Bobby!"

I will hear it again and again and again in my dreams. Their unearthly screams.

This note of pure panic triggered my first adrenaline rush. When that hits, you don't think—you DO. And you DO in a kind of controlled, warp-speed slow-motion. I was with "the force." My senses came alive.

As Dad and I waded out to get them, they were struggling, fighting. They had come in swimming from the other direction and now they were drowning. All for the want of the balloons. No reason to die. Inconsequential. They were screaming, fighting the weeds, screaming.

Dad couldn't swim a lick. He had some kind of water-phobia, was terrified of the depths. Despite that, magnificent in conquering his own fears, he waded in up to his neck.

Fortunately, I was part amphibian. I got to the young boy first. He, I like to think, was the most in trouble. Please allow me this leeway. Allow me the courtesy of believing me. After all, I allowed his sister to drown!

I have lived this experience once in reality, many more times in my mind.

The water wasn't even that deep—over their heads, but not a whole bunch. Panic, panic and the seaweed that's what was going to drown them. I got the boy, somehow, to my dad, and we got him to safety. I turned. Gone! Tears panicked in me. Out-of-control fear. Swim—dive down—swim—dive down—look! Where is she? Got to find her! Dad's voice mixed with my physical exhaustion. Physical exhaustion and aching, physical fear. Aimlessly swimming in circles, walking where I could touch bottom. Gone.

The tide had turned and was coming in. Gone—as simple and as complicated as that.

I finally got grabbed and taken to shore. Can't remember much more; didn't think I remembered this much. Pretty painful stuff.

Later that night, after the tide came in, we saw the Coast Guard come, and the sheriff, small boats, dragging for her body with long ropes, grappling hooks on the end. Finally, sleep. The whole thing was a blur of feelings, fear, shock, exhaustion. Spiritual and physical exhaustion. Other feelings would surface over the years, just as drowned children eventually rise to be seen again.

I always say a silent prayer for Kristine when I visit the Bay. I'm still devastated. I cannot change even one second of this day. I accept.

It would be presumptuous to say that I wasn't proud of Dad. Heck, it's a wonder he didn't drown—he must have felt that he'd buried himself in liquid death up to his chin! I was also proud of my part. I guess I was a hero.

I received the Royal Canadian Humane Society Medal for bravery. I was hot news. Lots of publicity, pictures in the paper, pretty heady stuff for a boy turned twelve.

Funny thing. Everyone always told me how good we had done. But no one ever asked how I felt about it.

Dad and I never really talked, either. He was proud of me for sure. I was proud of him. Shit, I wish we would have vented this out. Too late now; Dad's been gone since 1969. I wanted to hug him and tell him how proud of him I was. He was a hero, too.

But I got to be the celebrity.

If memory serves, it was a few days before the body was recovered. Crabs eat dead things; they are scavengers. God, I had some bad dreams. Bullshit—I had nightmares! Gut-wrenching nightmares! To this day, I've never been back to that side of Birch Bay at low tide. I put this behind me years ago. WE DIDN'T GET THEM BOTH!

THAT'S HOW I FELT! WHEN IT WAS TWO A.M. AND I COULDN'T SLEEP. ANGRY, INADEQUATE...

I got over it. Time heals. God willing, we will be at The Bay next summer, too. I'll do my prayer. Life will go on.

This incident opened many doors for me in the Royal City. And every time a door opened, my honest feelings stepped a little farther back into the shadows. Like Lon Chaney, I learned to be a man of many faces.

Excitement seems to be a component of my life, though. Things continually happen around me. Over the ensuing years I saved three more lives. Quietly on these occasions, with no fanfare. They all know who they are.

I know that none of them are this girl, Kristine.

My daughter, Trish, and her boyfriend, Les, recently experienced this phenomenon—of things happening around me—first-hand. We were at the beach in Kihei, Maui. The ocean was wild. We were sitting on the sand, just watching. I know where my balls are, now; the shore-break was just too big, too hairy, to risk injury. Bobby is growing up. (About time, so Pat says.)

We were watching some really dumb haoles in the water.

When Hawaiians talk about tourists, the nomer "haole" is not necessarily a good thing. Letting your children go into this kind of surf is typical haole behavior. Not even being there to watch them drown is also haole behavior.

Suddenly, a young girl from Australia was in a world of trouble—knocked off her feet by a large set of waves and pulled out by the undertow, right in front of us. Tricia screamed, "She's drowning!"

Les and I were already up and racing to the exposed lava rock that the riptide was pulling her towards. Les went the ocean way, and I went in through the rocks in front of her. As that great American philosopher Yogi Berra would say, "It's *déjà vu* all over again."

While Les was struggling to come up to her from behind, the child put a death-grip on some rocks, but each wave knocked her off and really banged her around. The old guy, me, was getting beat up pretty badly in the rocks, too. But at least she was being driven somewhat towards me. Suddenly absolute terror filled my voice as I screamed to Les to watch his back. A huge set of waves was coming! Les knew what to do—duck under and hang on.

The first wave dislodged the girl, knocked me ass-over-tea-kettle, smashed my elbows, and ripped off a chunk of my big toenail. But now the girl was closer. Finally Les and I made the exchange. The child was terrified; me, too! I'm getting a little long in the tooth for this stuff.

We got bounced around getting into shore. The poor little girl was ripped from my grip by the force of the waves; only for a second, though, and then she was in front of me, struggling towards the safety of the beach. Another man got involved. I passed the child to him and turned to find Les. He'd been carried back into the rocks. God hates a coward! I returned to help Les, and together we got smashed into safety.

I was down on one knee, staying as calm as I could, checking to see if the little lady hurt anywhere. We had a towel wrapped around her, and she was shivering from fear, close to shock. Out of nowhere her dad appeared. He didn't know what had just happened. Embarrassed, he just grabbed his daughter and took off down the beach.

Pat is a feisty wifey. She, all five-foot-one-inch of her, was chirping at the guy as he went down the beach: "My son-in-law... my husband... saved your daughter's life..."

Les and I were doing an inventory for hurts, and we looked at each other. We smiled. He knew now what it was like to have "the force." We both started laughing at Pat and limping back to the towels. Both of us were bruised; so was the guy who'd come in after we got her almost to safety. Handshakes all around. This was definitely a boy thing. Big toe was bleeding, but I had bigger fish to fry. Pat, the "whirling dervish," was back.

All's well that ends well; the man came over and thanked us. His daughter did, too. She hugged Les and me. It was a Kodak moment.

Now we both have a little girl in Australia who thinks we are "okay Canucks." She got a big scare on Maui, and I know she has respect for the ocean now. I have always loved the water. Could have something to do with having been in the amniotic sac. I feel at peace in the sea. Always have felt an affinity for the ocean.

This may sound morbid, but—like the whales, who were once terrestrial and returned to the sea, so shall I. After I'm cremated, Pat has agreed to place my ashes in the ocean off the coast of Maui.

I will be at peace there.

Normal Drinking Canadian Dude

Sometimes far too much emphasis is put on the word "normal." Growing up, we drank a lot. The concept of designated drivers didn't exist. Most of my friends drank the way I did—too much. One of my friends is now a judge; two more are successful lawyers. There's a school principal, an accountant, and an airline pilot. Only two of us are divorced. Alcohol was the reason in both cases—mine was one, of course. The wife of a dear friend also became an alcoholic.

Normal?

With keen observation skills I monitored the blossoming of Annette Funicello's breasts on *The Mickey Mouse Club*. Mine was the age of the ageless pimple-curer Dick Clark and his *American Bandstand*. Of *Rebel Without a Cause*—a great flick. Of *Beach Blanket Bingo*—a dog of a movie. (The only thing that could have saved it is if they'd started swapping partners). I learned that candy may be dandy, but liquor is quicker. I followed the Motown sound, Jerry Lee Lewis (now *there's* a piece of work!), Fats Domino, Smokey, Chubby... After I saw the movie A Summer Place, I bought me a red sweater just like Troy Donahue.

Tab "Let's go on a moonlight swim" Hunter couldn't sing at all. Me neither, but we both had blue eyes and blond hair. The similarity between me and Tab became part of my closing technique with the girls.

God, was I ever in a rush for sex! I don't mean that I rushed the act; I just wanted to buzz like a honey bee from flower to flower. I was disgustingly preoccupied with the whole subject. So were all my closet-masturbating friends.

The biggest fear, without question, was knocking a girl up. In fact, the black market in rubbers was a lucrative business. You were willing to pay top dollar to avoid buying them over the counter. And if you did go into the drug store, you waited until there were no females around—including the staff. Even so, the druggist always knew what you were doing. Often a guy would choke at the critical moment of asking. Imagine. Just barely able to mumble something inane, then bolting for the door.

The thought of "missed periods" still haunts my libido. But what the hell—it was an occupational hazard of my chosen avocation.

I'll tell you what, though. At one time, two "missed periods" by my main squeeze cost me pretty dearly. I developed alopecia areata, a nervous condition that caused me to lose my hair in patches. I shaved my head completely bald in my senior year of high school. I had to. By then, there were more patches than hair.

The alopecia was caused not only by the two missed periods but also by a near-death experience at the weekend job I had in the lumber mill.

I worked in the "power house" where we made steam for domestic power. The fuel was sawdust—shavings from the planers and hog-fuel bark from trees. This fuel was stored in a huge structure called "the bin," a concrete box one hundred feet high, three times that wide, and four times that in length. My buddy Garry and I shared the job of "binman," which was to scurry around inside that gargantuan building like two fleas in a dumpster, making sure that mountain-ranges of sawdust kept falling evenly into a subterranean chain system that dragged the fuel into the boilers. It was a dangerous environment. In fact, instability of the loosely packed fuel had cost another binman his life, and I came within a hair's breadth of sharing his fate.

We worked the night shift on the weekends. By that point in the weekly routine, the bulk of the main pile had already dropped through the floor, leaving fuel clinging to the interior walls in towering cliffs twenty or thirty feet high. My job was to stab at these cliffs with a fifteen-foot pole and make them avalanche. Garry's job was to spot for me and yell if he saw trouble coming. It was an insane situation. I could smell the risk, almost taste it. The danger of it felt like a weight on my back. God, I loved it!

This time, though, I didn't hear Garry's warning. Maybe he lost his footing for an instant and got distracted. Whatever happened, he couldn't see it fast enough—the whole cliff leaned forward and started to let go. I looked up. It was on me. I screamed and panicked, and then it smacked me square in the chest as I kept screaming, falling backwards into blackness and into the shifting, pressing weight of an avalanche of living, moving fuel.

It began with a tremendous explosion of kinetic energy. I fought with every fiber in my being. However shortly after this initial burst of trying to live, a calm acceptance came over me. I felt almost removed from all the banalities of what was going on in the sawdust. All that panic about up and down, would they pull me out head-first or legs-first? Now, what the hell did it matter? I was fucking gone, man.

When Garry saw me disappear, he made all the right moves. He threw the emergency switch, which shut off the machinery that would have dragged me down through the floor and crushed me further into the sawdust. The switch also set off an alarm that brought Bill, the engineer on shift, running. I was gone, completely unconscious, when, by pure shit-house luck, they were able to dig me out. They were stabbing wildly with pitchforks. I felt a prong pass right through my boot, between the leather and the skin. I saved that boot for years as a souvenir.

Then there was light.

I remember trance-like them clearing my air passages, me vomiting, seeing light, passing out again, riding in an ambulance, the wailing of a siren. I distinctly remember asking them to please just take me home. My father was the personnel manager and safety officer, and he had hired me. I didn't want to screw up his safety record. Then I passed out again.

I remember nothing of the emergency room, only a few flashes of intensive care. Kind nurses. I came around the next morning. I was in hospital for about a week. They had to do a technique called "postural drainage." This procedure consisted of elevating my rear while I knelt with my head over the side of the bed. A physiotherapist beat on my back, and this encouraged me to cough up sawdust from my lungs. After each one of these sessions I was exhausted from the beating and coughing. The desired effect was accomplished—I coughed up fluid and sawdust—but it was hard bloody work.

Because I'd screamed when I found myself buried alive, I had sucked sawdust into my entire respiratory system. I had reacted in stupid panic. Weeks later Garry told me that my scream had enabled him to get a bearing on where I was buried. Fear is good! Panic, too!

But I still don't like confined spaces. Pat also knows that I want to be cremated, not buried. Been there; done that.

The experience taught two lessons. First, it cured me of any fear of death. Just before I lost consciousness—in that state of indescribable peace—I realized that death doesn't hurt. And second, it taught me when I went back to the binman's job two weeks later that I could face the demons. I don't mind telling you, though, that I was never really comfortable in the fucking bin again.

Bob also grew up a bunch, a big bunch. I learned that the best part of life came despite fear or perhaps because of it. As a result *"joie de vivre"* rooted itself firmly in my soul. From that point on, I was almost reckless with enthusiasm for life—gusto, or nothing doing. I found myself jumping off a little higher than was safe, swimming farther out from shore than necessary, sleeping less than anyone else, driving my car faster than the speed limit, pursuing the opposite sex relentlessly, and drinking more than my peers. I had a fierce desire to succeed, to win, to be the last one standing. I was a doer—fun to be around, the one who made things happen.

Is this where my junkie personality emerged? Was this when my desperate intensity emerged, looking for something as powerful and purely dangerous as that avalanche of fuel that would help me cope with the raw risk of staying alive? "Shoots"—looking back is easy.

Still, somewhere around this time: enter the Witchy Bitch. Stage right. Slowly, at first. Inevitably, at the end.

There is a footnote worth mentioning. Approximately a month after the avalanche incident I started to cough in a high-school classroom. Big-time coughing, major league. The teacher sent for the nurse. I brought up a chunk of sawdust about the size of a large kernel of corn. Don, a weird friend, asked me if he could have it for his collection. He had his own tonsils in a jar of formaldehyde, his father's appendix likewise, and all his own primary teeth. Wonder what happened to that guy? Probably works for the government. Say in the income tax department.

What a hoot!

As I said, the hair went in patches. I had really nice hair, blond and curly, ducktail, the whole works. What happens with alopecia is that the scalp closes over the hair follicle, the follicle dies, and the hair falls out. Some people lose the whole enchilada—eyebrows, pubic hair, the works. I only lost the hair on my head in mangy-looking zones. Initially I was able to cover most of the bald spots with my remaining hair. But as my weird condition advanced, it created some interesting adventures.

For example, my head became a canvas in art class.

We called the art teacher "Floppy Tits." She was a really nice person, but we were convinced that she got her make-up from "The House of Pancake" and her perfume from "The House of Dunk-Yourself-In-It." (What cruel little shits we were!) Another buddy, Jim, who later went on to much success in a commercial art career, suggested that he customize the bald spot. He painted a bloodshot eyeball. The masterpiece was concealed under my ducktail.

The next class was social studies. This teacher, we'd decided, had the face of a walrus and a "bowling-pin physique." He had two particular methods for emphasizing the key points of his lectures—one was a knuckle to the head; the other was pulling a tuft of hair. This kind of "touch therapy" was normal behavior for teachers in those days. They could even hit you and not lose their jobs. (I personally feel okay with this type of discipline.) After getting seated, I flicked the ducktail out of the way to impress the "young tightie" behind me, and she lost it laughing. Great tits, but no brains! The Walrus approached. He knew I was involved in the disturbance, but he didn't know how. So he grabbed my hair. Without even trying, he pulled out a good-sized fistful.

His face turned a color of red that I've never seen since. He started panting and hyperventilating—I thought he was going to die! So I confessed. (Cruel nicknames aside, I really liked the old guy.) I explained about the alopecia, and that it wasn't his fault. Mercifully, he started to breath normally again, and his color returned. Life went on.

After this incident, I had a special relationship with this teacher. As I said, Jake was a pretty good old fart, but he never pulled my hair again. In fact, he never had the opportunity because, right after this incident, my friends and I all got drunk and shaved my head bald. But that's another story.

The amazing part about alopecia is that the hair almost always grows back. The root is okay; it's just the hair that falls out.

Mine grew back, too, after about a year—a different color now, and not as curly. Ask me if I cared what color it was, as long as it was real and it stayed put. And that little Delilah started getting her monthlies again, so eventually, like Samson, Bobson regained his locks. Cool!

The setting for this "normal" adolescence was a small town outside Vancouver British Columbia. Realistically the story could have taken place anywhere in the Pacific Northwest. Vancouver, Bellingham, Seattle, Portland are all same-same to me. I regarded the US State Patrol Troopers with the same healthy respect (and a tad of fear) that I feel for the "horse-men," our Royal Canadian Mounted Police. You don't choose to mess with these guys. As I said before, fear is good. So is respect.

The universality of alcoholism doesn't respect our undefended border. The founders of AA are American. In fact, culturally speaking, the dividing line between Canadians and Americans is a myth. Eighty percent of Canadians live within three hundred miles of the border, which they cross freely both in thought and in fact.

For example, I knew Joe Kapp, who came out of U.C.L.A. to play for the B.C. Lions. Joe went on to a hell of a career in Minnesota, playing with the Vikings. More recently, Warren Moon, who came out of the University of Washington, led the Edmonton Eskimos in the Canadian Football League to five consecutive Grey Cup championships before going south to fame and All-Pro status in the NFL.

I'll mention another former Heisman winner—not Joe Thiesman, although he played up here, too. The dude I am referring to is Doug Flutie, the Most Valuable Player in the CFL three years in a row. I saw the Seattle Seahawks play in the King Dome lots of times. Steve Largent was one of my favorite receivers. He was too small, too slow, but he earned All-Pro mainly by hard work and determination.

Jerry Rice is a different case. He has great wheels—can cut at warp-two—and the hands of a brain surgeon. He works just as hard as Largent did, but he's five inches taller and he can jump like Michael Jordan. The fact that Joe Montana and Steve Young were pitching him the old pigskin didn't hurt either, but make no mistake—Rice is one for the ages.

Dick Butkus is another one for the ages. Ray Nithche had a great relish for touch-therapy type tackling—a make-the-ball-car-rier-pay-in-pain work ethic.

Mickey Mantle finished his career playing for Seattle, I think. I feel confident that I saw him play there towards the end of his magnificent career. Can't remember for sure; it's been a long time. Besides that, the seventh-inning stretch was usually the end for me. By that point in the game I was totally pissed. American beer is "fucking-A."

Mickey himself finally died of a liver-rejection problem after receiving a transplant. Truth is, Mickey was a functioning alcoholic. His plea to the young was to "emulate the way I played, not my lifestyle." How good would he have been without the booze?

Talent and booze...

The grand witch Ethyl A seems to take special pride in hunting down the extraordinary people. For them she uses all her many hooks and spells. For simplicity's sake, Ethyl's pantry includes speedballs, coke, crystal meth, crack, heroin...Most addicts, and almost all alcoholics, start the adventure of addiction with Ethyl. She is easily secreted from your parents' liquor cabinet. Later you progress to your drug of choice. That's why, for the purposes of this text, any drug from booze to heroin comes originally from Ethyl's pantry. The music industry: Presley, Joplin, Hendrix, Morrison. The Hollywood Death Syndrome (mixing sleeping pills and booze): Marilyn Monroe, John Belushi, River Phoenix, Chris Farley. It's a long, long list, growing daily.

American and Canadian culture: same-same. I, too, know exactly where I was on November 22, 1963. I, too, was angry and shocked at the end of Camelot. December seventh, the day of infamy. July fourth, Independence Day. More Americans killed in the Civil War than all the others combined. Vietnam, Somalia, Bosnia, and the Gulf. The books by Colonel David H. Hackworth, the most decorated living American warrior. *Hazardous Duty* is a masterpiece.

Yeah, I have a lot of cross-culture, eh! Damned proud of it, too, eh! Canadians talk funny, eh? Just for a heartbeat, listen to someone from Boston, New York, the rural South, or Hawaii—and then we'll agree on who talks funny, eh! One of my favorite sports is basketball, eh!—invented by a Canadian, eh!

Enough already. We have so much in common as North Americans. Our two great democracies have social, economic, religious, and political similarities. We even have the longest undefended border in the world. As I said, I am just a normal Canadian dude with a universal disease called alcoholism. There is no cure, and I will always be in recovery. Normal for me is the same normal for you. That's the point. That's what I want you to see.

The border between me and you, Bob and boB, Mickey the Mighty and Vincent the Vulgar, is also an undefended border that anyone can cross without hindrance. One of the significant differences between Canada and America is that our rye whiskey is a whole bunch better than your sour mash corn liquor called bourbon. Yabba Dabba Do—eh!

Want to know why Canadians say "eh?" Spell "Canada."

C, EH, N, EH, D, EH.

So now you're enlightened, EH?

Rhapsody for Ethyl

Hindsight is twenty-twenty. When you're an emotional cripple, you're the last one to know. I was vulnerable after my first wife presented me with our son and only heir. I was already a heavy drinker even then, when my prince—eighteen inches long and seven-pounds-eight-ounces of fighting fury—was born on August 24, 1969. He was both the start and the finish of the baseball team that I wanted to sire.

The trauma of her baffling disease put me over the top, big time. She handed me the first thing in my life that I couldn't handle. By the demise of the marriage, I was well on the way to chronic alcoholism. Simply, I was unable to cope.

Multiple sclerosis is the biggest crippler of young adults in North America. I spent hours at the library internalizing every scrap of information that I could find about the illness. Then I went to the university library for more information. I wrote the Mayo Clinic in the United States for more information. Eventually, I learned to hate my wife for becoming sick. For ruining my life. God, was I bitter.

In time as the disease progressed, and it always does, I had a vasectomy. Bob kept getting his wife pregnant. The doctors would not allow us to have any more children. My baseball team was being aborted, one position at a time. Finally I gave up on having sex. I was devastated—to feel like a eunuch with my own wife, for God's sake. My finicky hair betrayed me again. Within six months, I was almost completely gray.

But, good grief, she was the one with the illness! The disease didn't cause me any physical pain. My wife was legally blind, suffering other motor-function loss, and I was powerless to help. Numbness in her hands caused her to drop things. Her legs were numb, and she stumbled and fell often. She was trying to cope— not well, but trying. For example, when she poured tea, she kept a finger inside the cup to let her know how full it was. The doctors gave her injections of a steroid-like cortisone to reduce the inflammation that was causing her vision to fail. It was extremely difficult to see her at the ophthalmologist, to hold her hand, as Doctor Harris stuck needles directly into her eyes. But for me the suffering was invisible and so, perhaps, much more serious than an external ailment—anger and fear. Why me? I knew that multiple sclerosis would only get worse. Sometimes a little knowledge is not a good thing. Men in general, I was to learn, do not cope very well when their wives become ill.

Sure, I put on a great front—for a period of time, anyhow. Inside I was bankrupt. I coped by using alcohol. I was a human cavity ready, willing, and able to enter into a "Fatal Attraction" affair with my nemesis, Ethyl.

Ethyl Alcohol.

As I said, I was already a functioning alcoholic by the time the real challenges began. It's a moot point when, or even if, I would have crossed the line into chronic alcoholism. If wishes were fishes and the Queen had balls, we'd all be singing "God Save The King."

The disease is progressive. I crossed the symbolic, invisible line into chronic alcoholism. Shit, I tripped over it—me being drunk, and it being invisible. I was always blessed with bigger balls than brains.

The great omnipresent Bob, Birch-Bay hero, athlete extraordinaire, young lion of the real-estate profession, youngest member of the million-dollar-sales club, successful businessman, was about to meet a real piece of work called Ethyl. Ethyl Alcohol is the name; booze is her game.

In retrospect it was no contest. I was doomed from the beginning.

The "for better or worse" part of the marriage vows had been broken already. Being a handsome young stud, I now qualified as an adulterer. This behavior caused more guilt. The guiltier I felt, the more I drank.

Ethyl and her promise of oblivion! The numb place only she could take me, a place where I wasn't afraid, a place where I was asexual, didn't hurt, didn't care. Until the morrow. Daylight always dropped me off back at the place where I couldn't cope. You get so you want to change the color of daylight. I had to be numb so that I wouldn't feel the pain, show the anger. Had to continue the charade. Ethyl, Ethyl, Ethyl—repeat as a mantra as you consume three doubles. Her calming touch replaces the unaccountable anxiety. Everything goes into perspective. Vindictive fantasies replace reality. Guilt disappears.

So do I.

I've always given the impression of taking up much more space than I actually do. But as this affair continued, the feeling of physically shrinking kept entering my conscious mind. These were uncharted waters for me. Fear of inanimate objects—a ringing telephone, for example—would cause an almost overwhelming panic. Fear and panic were my companions now, by choice. I was a loner.

Now that Ethyl had whetted my thirst, I had to keep heading for new watering holes. After all, I was a businessman. Couldn't have the bartenders thinking that I had a problem! Other patrons might also notice that I was there too often. Had to continue the charade. I still had my vestiges of self-esteem. Sure, Bob. Who was I kidding?

The reality was that everyone knew what was going on. Hell, I was making snow-angels at the reception of my best friend Mac's wedding. I passed out and had to be driven home. Normally, because I was always trying to keep up the storefront of normality, I didn't let myself get that out of control. I had an enormous capacity for drinking without acting drunk, but the emotion of my failure in marriage manifested itself in the behavior I displayed at the wedding.

Twenty years later, Mac said, "We all knew. But we didn't know what to do. And then, poof, you disappeared off the face of the earth."

By this point I was unable to function without Ethyl—and that fact filled me with even more guilt and self-loathing. Imagine

Bob the Omnipresent, totally beaten! Of course, I'd never admit it, not at this stage; boB still had miles to go before he slept. Nonetheless, to the victor go the spoils. Ethyl was the victress; alcohol my personal *Achilles' Heel*. I was expelled from paradise into the hell and slavery of addiction. In *Paradise Lost* Milton said, "Tis better to reign in hell than serve in heaven." I say bullshit. My time on the skids was hell. Hell sucks!

But she's only a woman.

Here's what I used to think, back when I was stupider: a real man could handle her! Male ego once again flexes its immature muscles.

The arrogance of the immature male mind sometimes causes me pain. I think back to high school and college years. The macho babbling of insecure boys' fragile egos, expounded while imbibing. The Four-F Club. Find 'em, feel 'em, fuck 'em, forget 'em. If they are old enough to bleed, they are old enough to butcher. Turn them upside down and they all look the same. What nonsense! What a bunch of closet masturbaters we all were. Meanwhile, I was becoming a terminally sick man.

God's gift that "gladdens the heart" is, for some of us unfortunates, a life sentence in the service of Ethyl Alcohol. She is a demanding, sordid bitch of a mistress. She's the most powerful solvent ever created. Her forte, like all solvents, is to remove things—marriages, families, bank accounts, and driver's licenses. Anything that the human condition can create, hold dear, and strive to attain. This she can do like no other.

She is a killer. She is insidious, cunning, baffling, and all-powerful to those caught in her web of addiction. She is even legal. The Volstead Act (the Fifteenth Amendment to the US Constitution) that ended Prohibition and allowed the establishment of organized crime, also meant that the lady was here to stay. Fact is, illegal booze financed the creation of organized crime. If this is God's gift that gladdens the heart, it only serves to prove that God has a sense of the bizarre.

If she were given proper credit as a cause of death, she'd rank up there with handguns and cancer. A drunk passes out in a flophouse while smoking. Fifteen people are asphyxiated—in other words, murdered. A drunk driver hits a family of five. Head trauma, internal injuries, coma, five deaths. That is to say, five murders. Spooky stuff.

What Ethyl really needs is more credit for her carnage. Statistics are neglectful in overlooking her. I can say this, being one of her disciples. But wisdom doesn't come easily, nor is it easy to pass on. Fully given credit, alcoholics cause a staggering amount of carnage—incest, rape, robbery, the list is endless. The cost to society is astronomical. Jeffrey "the Cannibal" Dahmer admitted that he had to drink to do the unspeakable deeds. In my case, though, I can honestly say that Ethyl enhanced the desire but took away the performance. That statement summarizes my blossoming relationship with Ethyl.

She went on to betray me. Left me like a cheap piece of ass with a hooker. Left me with a dose. The illness she left me with is as debilitating as AIDS, and as equally lethal. There is a cure, though, for alcoholism. Few make it. Most become unfortunate casualties in a no-win situation. Most go down muttering, "Rehabilitation is for quitters!"

Make no mistake: This isn't snakes and ladders. This ain't Monopoly. The "Go directly to jail" might apply, but forget the fucking two hundred dollars. You are in the big leagues now, sport. The ante in this game is your life. You're a dead bottlehopper walking. Choose to do something about your disease. Or die!

Bob Turns Himself In

My parents always considered the police to be their friends. They drilled the idea into our heads when we were kids, and I still live by that belief today. So the last semi-sane thing I remember doing was trying to get the police to put me in the drunk tank.

I'd never been in one before. I figured it was where I belonged.

The Bob personality was still around, but the contrary boB of the dark side, my Darth Vader personality, was becoming more dominant. The fictional Mr. Hyde, who had a doctor for a companion, shared many traits with the emerging boB, who had only me. Both of these dudes drank an elixir; as a result, both experienced profound personality changes.

The scene was early in the seventies, in the fall. Probably 1973. The years seem to mix together as in a daiquiri.

Not that it has any more significance than the size of mouse nuts, but the exact date of this event can be found easily by any one of my lawyer friends. If I had hired a lawyer, ironically the whole episode would have been settled differently. In fact, though, this mystery trip I'm about to describe resulted in the first and only entry on my criminal record.

To fully understand the story, you need to imagine (if you dare) my deteriorating condition. I was waiting in a hotel for a cab to take me the fifteen miles from New Westminster to the skid-row police station in Vancouver. My reasoning for going to another city? Simple. I didn't want anyone I knew to see me. Although my self-esteem was frayed, I still had vestiges.

But I was afraid and suicidal.

I was an empty shell. Separated. Wife and son gone. House gone, car gone, job gone, emotionally bankrupt. I'd been drinking for days—alone in a hotel room, not eating.

The year before, I'd sliced my wrist and got away with it (in the sense of not being locked up) by telling the doctor at the emergency ward that "the knife slipped while I was putting a Christmas toy together." I doubt he really believed me, but he let me out anyway. What I should have said was, "Help me, please. I'm a certified mentally-ill nut case." My Lon Chaney, man-of-many-faces personality was about to put me on the street; my wits were going to keep me there.

I had a mental image of an alcoholic, a skid-row dweller—dirty, wine sores, drinking weird stuff like after-shave, sleeping under bridges, sleeping in abandoned cars, a bloody disgrace. "Well, sir," I promised myself. "That's where I'm heading." What the mind can conceive, the man can achieve.

Get this! Around the time of this story I stole a bottle of Aqua Velva after-shave lotion. Not because I didn't have money. And not because I needed a drink—I had two bottles of Canadian Club in my hotel room. I stole it to see if I could steal. I stole it to practice drinking it. Because that's what I perceived alcoholics did. Down deep, I knew. God, I was naive! Full of false pride. I was like a lamb looking for a place to be slaughtered.

The Judas Goat was Ethyl. My witchy bitch of a mistress.

I didn't know that the desired method of drinking this stuff is to shake it into a glass, dilute it with water, then "prost"—down the hatch. You have to hold your breath because of the gag reflex. You breathe through your nose—you've got no taste buds in your nose, not unless you're half Vulcan or full Romulan. (That's an attempt at levity, sort of comic relief. For my own sake. I still have trouble visiting these times even in my memory. God! I was a mess! Pitiful and sad.)

I shook the after-shave into my mouth directly from the bottle. Yuck, that was awful! Every drop burned its way down my gullet. Talk about the death of a thousand cuts! But I was a gamer, came to play. I puffed my chest in an attempt at being macho. Finally I puked my guts out.

Practice makes perfect. boB was on a mission.

Slowly, painfully, I was learning to be "street wise." What a profound waste! In retrospect, boB "the contrary" was mostly in charge now, hell-bent to tackle this broad called Alcohol. Forgive him, Lord. The silly, sick, stupid boB knew not where he was going. He was starting his journey from vodka to vanilla.

High noon was approaching, and this poor silly alcoholic was going to find out about being forsaken—big time. If any of you kids at home are thinking of trying this, please don't. Chances are it will Fucking Kill You. Can you say that word? Can you spell the word KILL?

I wanted to turn myself in because today I had wet the bed for the first time ever. Too much booze and no food. I'd started dreaming that I was going to the bathroom and then woke up peeing the bed. A nocturnal emission of the kidney kind. I was disgusted. Ashamed.

I knew what lay ahead. Propping a chair under the mattress. Using a towel to sponge up the urine. Bed sheets hanging everywhere. Self-esteem further frayed. Vestiges fewer. Sleeping in the bathtub. Damage control, sort of.

More likely, totally out of control.

By now I had already fallen asleep with a cigarette smoldering on my chest. The burn was terrible. I still have the scar today. But that didn't bother me as much as today's cigarette burn on the coffee table in my hotel room. You can't let anyone know! I'd spent the day scraping the coffee table to eliminate any traces of burn. Then I worked cigarette ashes and shoe polish into the scraped area. The bed was made and a full beer tipped over as though it was the cause of the dampness. A final touch of brilliance, *the piece de resistance*—an ashtray over the burned patch.

"Ring, ring goes the bell. Cook in the lunchroom ready to sell." Actually, it was the desk. The cab had arrived. *Thanks awfully, old man. Could you please have him come round to the parking lot? I have to go see a friend and need to get some things out of my car.*

Hell I didn't even have a car. The object of the exercise was to get to the cab without passing the registration desk. I was practicing to see if I could extricate myself from the hotel without paying the bill.

Pitter patter...
Ta ta, and so long sucker.

The ride to the police station was uneventful. I had a few shots in the cab; so did the driver. I almost left him the remains of the bottle as a tip, but then I decided not to. The prick didn't agree with my strategy, my major goal—incarceration. He tried his best to talk me out of it. Asshole.

Main and Hastings, everybody out. The heart of Vancouver's skid row. Headquarters of the largest police detachment in the city. All I had in my duffel bag was a second bottle of booze—this one unopened—some rumpled clothes, and about six hundred dollars in cash. My estate in fee simple. I slipped around the corner for one last GLUG. Better make it TWO. What the hell. ONE FOR THE DITCH.

I stashed the heel of the opened bottle. Didn't think it appropriate to carry an opened bottle into the police station. That would be illegal, wouldn't it? I figured I could get into the drunk tank without breaking any laws. Alcohol, my djinni of dreams, would take me anywhere I wanted to go. Let me live in my fantasy world.

The desk sergeant looked up and there was the Bottlehopper, looking a little rumpled in his Warren K. Cook sports coat and Dacks shoes.

"Excuse me, sir. I would like to be put in the drunk tank."

"Say what?" he replied.

"Incarcerate me, sir. I am drunk. Please put me in the drunk tank."

"Have you ever been in the drunk tank?"

"No sir, officer, sir."

He folded his arms across his portly chest and squinted at me skeptically. In those days, when I still had some measure of control, I looked okay on the outside. However, the view from inside looking out was another story.

"Why don't I get a patrol car to take you to a hotel in a safer part of town, and you can sleep this off. Phone a friend in the morning to come talk to you."

"NO sir, officer sir."

"People piss their pants in the drunk tank. They vomit. They shit themselves. You don't WANT to go in there."

"Yes sir officer sir. Suicidal, sir."

Round and round it went. No matter what I said, he wouldn't take me. Finally this kind man said, "I have work to do. Either you get drunker or commit a crime, or you don't get put in jail."

This cop and I had communication problems. He was getting a little snippy, calling my bluff.

Summoning as much dignity as possible, I asked if I could please use the "facilities."

"Sure," he said. "The shitter is down the hall on the left."

"Would you mind keeping an eye on my personal possessions," I asked, "while I visit the washroom?"

He eyed me curiously. I doubt his other clients used such expressions as "facilities" and "washroom." I was obviously green at this degenerate business. Get this—I washed my hands, straightened my tie, and buffed my shoes with the used paper towel before I came back for my duffel bag.

"Take care in this part of town," he said. "There are some really bad guys out there."

Silently I thought, *Fuck you*. And with as much dignity as I could muster, head high I left.

I retrieved the stashed bottle, had a giant hit, and looked for a safe hidey-hole. I had to do some strategic planning, internalize some information, and then put a plan into action. The bottle and the Bottle-hopper, like Siamese twins, joined at the lips. How insane was I? Totally unhinged!

The nerve of that fucking cop. GLUG. I pay his bloody wages! GLUG. Out-negotiated by someone who's still playing guns. What a fucking failure. GLUG, GLUG. Open the last fifth.

I had no idea at the time, but the events of the next hour were to set the tempo for the next six years of my existence. My existence then had no resemblance to a life.

The problem was getting incarcerated. I had tried drinking; it didn't work. The other option he gave me committing a crime didn't enter the picture. After all—crimes are against the law!

Smaller glugs. Now I was shit faced drunk...

Take another kick at the can. Back in I went. "Just following orders, slur."

Same sergeant.

"OSSsifur-slur, you can take me now."

"Get out of my fucking station house. Sit outside on the steps. I'm going to call you a cab to get you to a hotel. NOW!"

Screw you was my non-verbal reply as I retreated into the darkness. In retrospect, this man was a saint. But not then, not to me, not by a long shot. In my mind-set he was a fucking jerk.

But like John Paul Jones, I had not yet begun to fight. I left, back to the safety of my hidey-hole. Smaller glugs. "This fucker wants to play hardball." Play hardball with *me*! The fool!

Not just any crime, a *perfect* crime. I conceived the plan of venting my frustration by assaulting a police car.

It was a big ambition for a guy who had never done anything worse than get a couple of speeding tickets.

I smashed the remainder of my bottle against a brick wall. With single-minded purpose I made it to the police station's parking lot. I started looking for a weapon, a club of some kind. There was a metal sign bolted onto a bar of angle iron. I grabbed this staff of my soon-to-be sword of vengeance. Vigorously bending it back and forth I finally got it to snap off at the ground. Thus armed with my angle-iron lance, complete with its "No Parking" sign still attached, I went forth to slay the front windshield of a squad car.

It's hard to break a windshield, even when you're sober. I kept stabbing, but the iron kept slipping up the slope of the glass. Three times I struck, and then—smash! —the windshield exploded in a shower of fragments. The lance lurched through the broken glass. I stumbled forward, flopped onto the hood, then slid and fell to the ground.

INSANITY, I HAVE COME!

Using the bumper and the grill of the police cruiser, I pulled myself up, hand over hand, and dragged myself to my feet. Unsteadily, I balanced there with my hands extended.

HI HO, HI HO, IT'S OFF TO JAIL I GO.

HI HO, MY HANDS ARE FUCKING NUMB.

HI FUCKING HO.

YO!

Yo!

Where are these guys? No one's coming to arrest me. I'm barely ambulatory. You'd think a man could get a little help around here! Listen, we pay good, hard-earned, taxpayer's dollars to get arrested when we need to. But are the cops ever around when you need them?

No.

What are the odds? I've often wondered. *What's the probability of getting caught if you bust up a squad car in the parking lot of a major police station?* Astronomically high, methinks. But tonight, no such luck. I had to make it all the way back to the entrance on Main Street, and negotiate the stairs. Same sergeant on the desk. He noticed that I was packing a lot more of a load, but he didn't believe me about the police car. I was having a bad hair day.

Finally the sergeant agreed to come out and look, but we didn't go back down the front steps. We went through the building. As a result, I was disoriented and couldn't find the police cruiser.

Imagine my feelings, the embarrassment, in front of my new friend. I explained that all good relationships are built on truth, trust, and mutual respect. I reassured him I was being truthful.

He was pissed.

I begged, "Please let me check this last row." SUCCESS! Imagine how proud I was to show my new friend my accomplishment.

Well, they took me then. But I never did get to the drunk tank. They put me in a sort of padded cell, took my belt, shoelaces, took a sample of my blood...

Then during the night a male psychologist came to see me, and then a female psychologist came to see me. I was booked and fingerprinted sometime during the night. I got to try on new kind of jewelry called handcuffs. Pointed out that it was really a misnomer, they should really be called "wrist cuffs." No one really cared.

The next morning I was in court. Charged with "public mischief." Pled guilty. Fined one hundred dollars and given sixty days to pay. The judge said in a regal tone, "You may have a problem with alcohol!" No shit, Sherlock. I thanked his Honor, retrieved my possessions—every penny of my money—and was released, all before noon. Slamb bam... Fuck you, lamb.

I crossed the street and went into a bar called the Savoy. Couldn't have gone into the Empress Hotel on the same side as the police station. No fucking way. That was the cops' bar. Apparently boB was several times over the drunk-driving alcohol level. I'd learned this information in court. The blood samples they took the night before had tipped them off to my condition. Talk about justifiable indignation! I was framed.

Glug.

I drank six quick beers. Fantasized that I was now like Dillinger. They would never take me alive. Perhaps I'd join the Foreign Legion—they took criminals—become a soldier-of-fortune. Kill people! Kill cops! I'd only done what the cop sergeant had told me to do. I wanted to get put in jail. He told me to go commit a crime, so I did. And now here I was. And they were ripping me off for a hundred dollars. The injustice! I paid their damned wages. I was a tax-paying citizen.

"Miscarriage of justice," I muttered as I stood having a pee. Shitter. This place is a shitter. Not a washroom. Dillinger doesn't wash his fucking hands. *"Got to find a liquor store,"* I thought. *"Buy some of the good stuff."* Getting tired of being the middle man with beer. Half my life was spent with my dick in my hand. Beer's only good for maintaining the numb space. To make a numb space, it's hard liquor.

I believe that was the day boB "the contrary" became dominant. At any rate, I lost bladder control around this time. With this loss, another fragment of my being disappeared.

The other Bob was still around, shaking his head a lot. He became like an appendix, a vestigial organ. A recessive gene. Didn't do anything; he was only along for the ride.

The primary goal of the drunk tank had not been accomplished. I had stormed the Bastille, though. Liberty, Equality, Incarceration! Setting goals, having an action plan and being focused does work. Persistence pays off.

The glass was always half-full in those days. I thought *"quenching the thirst helped me think."* And I was going to achieve my ultimate goal of the drunk tank many times in the years to come. Under duress.

As the first cop said, "You don't want to go in there. The drunk tank is not a very nice place." But that's another chapter in this saga of self-destruction.

Street Wise

After leaving the Savoy, I hooked up with some of the good stuff from the liquor store and got myself a room in the Cobalt Hotel. Paid for two weeks up front. A single room with a sink. The shitter was down the hall, in a room all by itself. Next to that was a washroom with a tub and sink.

The walls of my room had cracks that ran from the floor to the ceiling. The floor, too, was a patchwork of cracked linoleum with cigarette burns and patches of dirty sub-flooring. The ceiling must have been fourteen feet high, and from it hung a scrawny cord with a naked bulb—the room's only illumination. There was a hot plate and a small fridge. Hospital-green walls under the light of that grim bulb created the perfect ambiance for vomiting.

I hung out in the bar downstairs and sipped on a few beers until I was ready to retire to the sanctuary of the room to do my serious drinking. This was my developing pattern. My main pastime was people-watching. When I was close to being drunk I finished the job in the sanctuary of the room.

I started a few friendships and heard about the Casual Labor Office, a program run by the provincial government. The location was close to the Cobalt. Actually within walking distance. The office was a large room like a union hall, complete with tables and chairs. Here the unemployed could find an opportunity to earn minimum wage doing manual labor.

Most of the work involved digging—digging new water lines after ancient galvanized pipes had burst, or digging up the perimeter of a home to replace drain tile. Sometimes it was warehouse work, where anything that could be consumed or stolen was fair game. Several times I worked in a candy warehouse—all kinds of chocolates. My blood-sugar level must have been off the scale. Other times they'd have me unloading a boxcar.

Thanks to the Casual Labor Office, I could make money working with a pint in me and a pint on me (safely tucked in the small of my back and secured by my belt). Ain't life great? boB's a lucky guy.

The ability to live in my memories was a necessary skill: put my mind in neutral and push. These were very physical jobs that required no expertise, just a strong back. Unfortunately there was a pecking order, and it wasn't guaranteed that you got work every day.

The true priorities for me were booze, shelter, and clothing. Like I said, time went okay for me because I knew how to work. Having been a superior athlete didn't hurt either. If I couldn't get out that day, card games like hearts and (my favorite) bridge filled the time. I was happy. I accepted my lot in life. Bob had chosen to be here.

I found out about the "Sally Anne Boutique" (the Salvation Army thrift store) and got hooked up with some work clothes. Mackinaw shirt with a tee-shirt under, and a couple of pairs of dark-green work pants. I also found out a trick—when I wet myself, the best thing to do was dampen the rest of my pants with water so that the color looked uniform. They dried evenly by body heat.

Tricks of the street.

And while I was adjusting to my new life, I was constantly on the prowl for safe places to sleep outdoors. I knew that eventually I was going to have to choose between booze and shelter. And I knew the choice I was going to make. I just hadn't found a safe place yet. Patience is a virtue, Bottlehopper.

My new life. Speaking as a consumer of booze, I had finally made it to the big time. I was no longer an amateur; I was now a professional alcoholic. Like a ballplayer who's worked his way up from the Double-A and Triple-A teams; like a Mafia stooge who's earned his bones and was ready now for acceptance into the family, I had completed my metamorphosis. I was hell-bent and guilt-driven to be a successful drunk.

Feel no pity for the Bottlehopper. I had always taken the advice of Yogi Berra, who said: "When you get to the fork in the road—take it!" This was yet one more act of total commitment. Over the next few years, my ambition for my new profession was just as they said in the television ad for the Army: "Be all that you can be."

Alcoholism, like marriage, is unconditional.

The Bottlehopper was expanding his horizons, learning to nourish his illness by experimenting with all sorts of exotic elixirs. Sterno is meant to keep fondues warm, but when it's strained through a pair of dirty socks or underwear to remove the camphor, it yields a liquid that can then be mixed with water and drunk. Bay rum, a type of hair tonic, can be consumed. So can Aqua Velva, rubby (rubbing alcohol), Scope mouthwash (runs eighteen percent on a hydrometer), Lysol (a cleaning disinfectant), perfume, and vanilla extract (the natural stuff a personal favorite).

One learned to adjust one's tastes according to two forms of pressure—the limitations of one's buying power and the necessity to imbibe. Of course, cost and ease of "boostability" always entered the equation, especially if one consumed what we called the exotic "drugstore stuff."

Here is an example of my thinking in those days: just because you're not paranoid doesn't mean you aren't being watched. Do you have irrational feelings of being followed, boB? Well, ya made it!

Clump! Clump! Clump! The noise of the clumping of my boots, this pulse of sound, encompasses my senses. The skill of being able to put my mind in neutral and push. This is something only the alpha predators achieve. The ability to keep going even when sick. That's what makes you a survivor. Learn to play with the small hurts. Prey are to be consumed—used to facilitate, and then discarded. Friends? I am my only friend.

The mind-set is to believe half of what you see, less of what you hear. You lower your standards and drink with pukes—but only if it's their booze. You earn the respect of your peers by giving "an guy entrance fee", (the price of one beer) getting him into the bar; then the rule is "Keep the hell away from me. I'm an okay guy, not a fucking mark." I paid to get them in the bar—let them hustle their own drinks now.

This sortie into the skids was a constant learning experience. The stakes were pretty high. I learned to observe, to develop a sense of nearby danger. Always sat with my back to the wall in a bar. To this day, there are only a few I would trust to protect my back in a confrontation; most of them are recovering alcoholics. Again, a paradox. The key word is "recovering."

Here's another trick of the street. The end of the month, when working-class men get their paychecks, is welfare time for drunks. In other words, it's a great time to hustle drinks, but you have to be cautious. Life is risky until everyone has consumed his pay check's-worth of booze. Mood swings, often instantaneous, explode into fisticuffs—and 'tis far better to deliver a sucker punch than to receive one.

I remember one Native Indian who was packing a real load early in a new month. He was drinking in the beer parlor, minding his own business. I was sitting with my back to the wall with my newspaper, blending into the scene. A native lady came in, spotted the man, and casually walked over behind him. She reached inside her purse, pulled out an almost-full fifth of wine, then smashed it over his head. Wow, what a sound! He went down as if he'd been pole-axed. The lady turned on her heel and left.

I thought the man was dead. Because I had an industrial first-aid ticket, secured back in my lumber-mill-job days, I was qualified to check the guy out. I made sure the waiter was watching my back. It made no sense for me to become another casualty. He had one large cut that would need ten stitches, and he had lots of abrasions. But he breathed normally. I wrapped and elevated his head while we waited for the ambulance attendants. Me, Mr. Nice Guy.

For the effort, I managed to cadge six free beers.

The key skill exhibited in the broken-bottle story? The fact that I had the waiter watching my back, protecting me. Take care of number one; if not, you learn not to bother. Let them be.

Morals? Doing good? Conscience? Get over it. I did. Steal a guy's wallet, then help him look for it. So I learned, and I survived. I paid this price for survival. I compromised old values. I learned to sing for my supper at the Sally Anne. The Sally also became my haberdasher. Contacts who were in treatment could "back door" me some clean clothes. Damp farts were a way of life.

Smart drunks learn to become territorial. If we venture too far from our safe flop, we are vulnerable. If we lose control too far from the sanctuary of the flop, we risk getting rolled, becoming prey, being scooped for drunk. There's genuine fear in a life like this. Panic!

For example, I was up in Gas Town in Vancouver, at the Travelers Hotel. Only ten blocks or so from the safety of the flop, but a mile too far. Had to find a temporary hidey-hole. This happened every time I fucked around with mixing booze and drugs. Did some weed, a couple of blue valium (ten milligrams), and a capsule of something—didn't know what, didn't care.

I found a ramp down by the waterfront, and crawled under. My plan was to pass out for three hours, void (the secret word), then wake up shivering and cold. Then check out my condition and, if okay, walk home to the flop. By the time I got there I'd be warm and the pants would be pretty much dry. At the flop, I had some medicine (booze) stashed so I could make it through the rest of the night.

It was pretty dark and spooky under there. Oh, well. It was kind of cozy, too.

Oblivion!

Then a sudden pain jolted me out of that drugged coma—a terribly sharp pain and a tugging sensation on my right cheek. I reached up, kind of confused. Blackness everywhere. Something heavy on my chest. An animal. A cat? My hand touched its tail. There was no fur on its tail.

Suddenly the thing let out a high-pitched, metallic-sounding SHREEEEK right in my face. I clutched my fist around its tail, which felt like a dry, stiff worm wriggling in my fingers. I pulled, and the thing shrieked again.

A goddamn RAT! A big one! Big enough to take down Benji the wonder dog—fattened on garbage and street filth, killer, predator king. Eating my face!

Nausea and horror flashed through my body. I went crazy. Got to get out. Where was I? Hemmed in by concrete wet and cold, like a premature burial. I convulsed and spun. Scampering on hands and knees, I raced toward a dim light, banging myself recklessly against concrete structural supports, and bouncing off wooden beams. Finally I shot out from under that ramp like a mad Italian circus star blasting out of a cannon. Boom!

I stood there in the darkness wiping my hands on my pants over and over, trying to rub off the feeling of the rat's verminous tail. Walking in circles. Cursing. My stomach was heaving, but I forced myself not to retch. I was raving—evil, filthy, rodent, rats, snakes, spiders... I hate them all and what a noise the rat made! Wow! Finally the reactions settled into an uncontrollable shivering. Perhaps I had an abrasion on my face and it had smelled the blood. Ugh!

I felt gingerly with my finger. He'd carved a chunk of flesh out of my right cheek, just below my eye. Fuck! Fear is the best sober-upper I know. Bleeding like a stuck pig. Funny thing how your own blood always looks like more than someone else's. A little knowledge is scary. Bubonic plague. Rabies! The blood kept coming. I wasn't coagulating. In those days I wasn't eating well enough or often enough to coagulate. I decided that I'd better walk to the emergency room at the hospital.

But then the gendarmes pulled over.

"You okay, buddy?"

"Yeah."

They shined their flashlight in my face. "Holy shit! What happened? Joe, look at the blood on this guy."

Obviously, this cop was a pussy.

So I sold them a bill of goods—how I'd been out drinking with a buddy, and we got separated. I got scared; that's why I ducked under that ramp. Get this: "I sure am glad you came along," I said. "I was alone and frightened, and then a big rat bit me, and I was on my way to a hospital, any hospital. Where's the closest one, please?"

"Get in the car, buddy. We'll take you to the hospital."

The poor guy cringed at the sight of my face as I slid into the back seat. Then he sparked up the lights, and off we went. What a hoot! No siren, but plenty of lights and speed. Those cruisers have balls when they're floored. While we ate up the roadway, he pulled out a first-aid kit and handed me some gauze and antiseptic. At the hospital a nurse speared me with the biggest fucking needle I've ever seen. Fortunately, she chose to skewer me in the ass—if they'd put it in my arm, I would have been flying on only one wing. But my ass was sore for a week. Thereafter, I had a numb bum.

They couldn't stitch it up; the missing chunk was the size of two-bits. I still have the scar on my cheek, and, like the slash scars on my wrists, I consider it a badge of honor. Told you I was made; I'm still earning my bones.

All that, and the cops didn't scoop me, either. God is good.

I bullshitted the emergency staff out of twelve dollars and some change and, all patched up, walked out carrying an envelope of free antibiotics. I reeked of antibiotics and the tetanus shot. Gave them a great story about being down on my luck while waiting for a check. What an asshole, Edwards! It was raining a little by then. I felt like I was in Gene Kelly's movie, "Singing in the Rain." Shuffling my feet to the vaguely remembered music, I found my way back to the viaduct.

Under the viaduct, I was safe. My flop. A little shivery. Time for a couple of shots of the real stuff. MY medicine. Just enough to get me back to sleep. Didn't want to piss myself again. That's a shitty way to start the day—correction, got to get it right—a pissy way to start the day. I am good at the panhandling. Glug! That's better. Glug! Glug! Stashed the money. Stashed the remaining booze. As the police sergeant said, there are some real bad asses out here.

For example, some are consummate liars. Like me, for example.

The Complete Predator

A year or so into the scene, boB has evolved. It's taken a concerted effort, plenty of physical labor, and a strong mind-set. Now he's a mean thirty-four-year-old fighting machine. He lives by his own personal theory of relativity, based on alcoholic reasoning and the reality of the street. Survival equals kick ass squared. boB follows basic rules. For example, predators survive; prey don't.

It's a nice fall evening around nine-thirty. I'm heading from the West Hotel, which is in my territory, to visit some friends in another territorial hotel, The Pacific. I'm only packing a small load. Just got a glow on. If I was packing a full load, I'd have been too drunk to walk straight. I would not have chanced going if I were vulnerable. Not only that, I'm flush. I scored forty bucks working. Thirty of those bucks are stashed in my boot. Everything is cool.

Walking east on Pender towards Main Street, I've got all my defensive shields in place. I'm "walking tall"—not aggressive, avoiding eye contact, just keeping aware, staying on the edge. Mild September evening. Just out to do a little socializing with some dudes I knew from Casual Labour. Just going to spend the evening with some company. The herd instinct, I imagine.

That's my first mistake. Here, you don't have any friends. If somebody wants to see me, they should come to *my* watering hole, on *my* turf.

So, even though I'm feeling good, I'm walking close to the curb where it's safer. Keeping open terrain between me and the dark caves of the buildings. All systems go.

Two longhairs walk towards me. Slumming? So it seems. They're dressed too well. Could it be just a couple of rich kids out for the night? But something's wrong. Bad body language. The big one, with the weightlifter arms. He's the worst, the dangerous one. The fucking puke is making fists—that's a curious signal. Being cautious, I'm quite prepared to leave the curb to avoid contact. But shit. Trouble!

I'm being blocked.

"What's up, guys?"

Their eyes are wrong.

"Like, man—give us your wallet."

I chuckle and say, "Do I look like I have a wallet?"

"Now, man!" the smaller guy says.

Thank God for peripheral vision. The big one with the arms is stepping into me for a sucker punch. Fuck. I step into his punch. His right glances off my forehead, above my left eye. Shit, that connected. He must have had fists of steel. But I hit him solidly, righteously. I got a surge of pleasure from it—the physics of a short left smashing full-force directly into his nose, combined with the kinetic energy of our two masses of energy colliding. Next to an orgasm, it's the greatest feeling.

Where is the other one? I was exposed at my back. For no reason other than panic, I step back and drop to my hands, kicking backwards low and hard. Boy, this is unbelievable—the other guy hadn't even moved. Things are happening at warp speed. Luckily, I got good boot-leather on his knee.

It's over.

The first guy, Muscles, was still down and out, duck-hunting with a rake. The prick! This other asshole was a pussy, crying and holding his leg. I take a swing at the whiner, but I pull the punch and hit him just hard enough to put him down. I only want to put him down. It's a stupid move, a Mother Theresa move, because I foul the punch and shatter my knuckles.

He went down submissively, but now I'm raging. I'm out of control. My knuckle hurts, so he will hurt. So it is written; so it shall be.

I kick the pussy in the ribs hard. Fucking stoked is the way I feel. STOKED. When Muscles' nose exploded, that was a Kodak moment. I could feel it pulsing, almost sensual, all the way up my arm. What a rush! I'm bleeding from my left eye. I stick my finger up to check the cut. It's numb. Sticky, not sore. Shots to the head are only numb. Strangely, they don't seem to hurt. On general principles, I kick the fucker in the leg. Don't want him to choke on the blood, so I turn him over. Another kick to the ribs. Suffer, you prick!

The little guy is still crying. He's pissed himself, and he's trying to get away. I grab him by the hair and give him a knee. Down he goes whining.

"Don't hurt me any more, man!"

Pure rage controls the next part—rage and justifiable indignation. There's no one around to help me. I've got to get these bastards arrested, and I'm going nuts because this guy's crying and he's still trying to get away. His leg, the good one, his femur, is jutting over the curb into the street and I jump on it.

His thigh-bone snaps. Crack! Simple as that.

Now he's quiet. Finally. Must have passed out. Good.

I raise my head to the darkness and beller a primal scream into the empty, trashed-out concrete canyon: "FUUUUUCK!"

Still no one around. My cut head is bleeding into my eye. With single-minded purpose, I walk one street over, towards Hastings—it's a busier street—to find a cop. I'm cussing. What does it take in this town to get a little assistance? Finally I spot a motorcycle cop sitting parked on his bike as if he's waiting for some lunatic to come walking out of the darkness. So I do, dripping blood and everything.

"These guys just tried to mug me," I tell him. So he drives around the corner while I cut back through a brick-strewn vacant lot. It's not far.

Both of my new friends are still there on the sidewalk where I left them. Muscles is making some noises now behind the blood streaming from his nose and mouth. "Want me to give him another shot?" I ask the cop. I actually make a fist. Ouch, that hurt. My knuckles are definitely not kosher. I have done some damage.

"Shit," he says. "Looks like a war zone. Sit down on the curb here, buddy," he says to me. "You're bleeding pretty bad."

He checks out the Dynamic Duo. Cuffs the big guy. He'll be okay—really sore, but okay. The other guy moans that his leg is broken, then passes out again. Then two patrol cars pull up, an ambulance, an unmarked car with two detectives. Everything is lit up just like a rock concert. The medic takes a look at my head and starts patching me up. "Five stitches, minimum" he says. "Make sure you get a picture of that right-hand knuckle when you get to emergency."

"What's the damage on the other two?" I ask in a concerned voice.

"The big guy is okay. Nose is flattened. Bone right through it. Nice shot. He's also complaining about his ribs. The other guy's not so good—bruised face, abrasions. On one leg, his knee's messed up. The femur on the other leg is broken for sure."

"I sort of figured that."

A young-looking detective interrupts: "Bob, get back to our car. We'll finish this report on the way to the hospital." As we walk to the car, he asks, "So how come you were so sure about the leg?"

"I stomped it on the curb," I say matter-of-factly.

"Bob," he says, "we want these two assholes, not you. Could you have possibly fallen in the struggle? Maybe you fell on that leg with your knee."

"Sure. It could have been like that."

"Any martial arts training?"

"No, sir."

"Any record?"

"Yes. Public mischief. No one got hurt."

As it turns out, these two "weekend warriors" have been working the strip for a month, hurting drunks, and taking their money. Now the cops have them—including the piece of pipe that the big one used inside his fist. The tail end of the pipe is probably what laid open my skull.

When you go to emergency with two detectives, especially if you're a good guy, you get the royal treatment. The doctor even freezes the cut before he stitches it up. (Six stitches—the medic was right.) "No real scar," says the doctor. "The cut's in your eyebrow." Tetanus shot in the ass. Then up to X-ray for a photo op. Three small knuckle-bones are cracked. "We can't put a cast on it, so it's just going to hurt." They give me a dozen two-ninety-twos for the pain, and a shot in the arm of something *real* good. What a hoot! I'm feeling good but thirsty. Always the thirst, pulling at me. Never leaves me alone, the thirst. The need is always there.

As I get ready to leave, the older cop, a porky-looking guy—his name is Bob same as me—says, "Bob, we have to ask you to come down to the station."

As we go to the car I tell him, "Look, I need a drink. I'm shaking like a bloody leaf. Cut me loose. I did my duty."

The younger cop, the smart one, says, "We'll get a pint, and you'll get a drink."

"That's a done deal, officer."

"What do you drink?"

"Vodka. The cheap stuff."

As I crack the bottle, I read the label—Smirnoff. The good stuff. Who will ever believe this? "This is cool," I say. "Drinking good vodka in a cop car." Glug, glug. Their treat, even. Unbelievable!

The Bob cop says, "Christ, only one drink and the booze is half gone!"

"Half full," I correct him.

The smarter dick says to me in a don't-screw-with-me voice: "Put it in your jacket." Then he lays out the situation. "We've got a bit of a problem here. The parents are in touch with the station. They want us to charge you for hurting their poor, young, under-age sons."

I scream, "Fuck—they attacked ME! They were trying to roll me! They thought I was drunker than I was."

"I told you. We want them, Bob—not you. We have to do this by the numbers or else they'll walk. Them being helpless children and all."

He says that last bit with a bitter grin.

"All I need is some of your time. We have other witnesses. There were many other victims. I want to nail these punks. They're both over eighteen, so they'll do real time. They had enough hash on them to charge them, and we will. But I want to get them for the muggings as well."

Then he looked at me.

"Trouble is, you really hurt them. You used excessive force. You broke one guy's leg. The doctor says he's going to have to operate and put a pin in the femur. We want to downplay your part and use the other victims."

"Those bastards attacked ME! They would have really hurt me! I didn't use excessive force. There were *two* of them. I was lucky. How did I know they weren't going to kill me? This isn't justice. This is unfair!"

"CALM DOWN, BOB! Now listen. When it goes to court, we probably won't be able to find you. After all, you're a vagrant." He winks. "But we need your statement. I want to run this by my boss in case I need any more paperwork from you. Hang in here with us. I give you my word that you'll be out in an hour."

The young cop is as good as his word. As I'm getting ready to leave, he hands me his card and says, "Tomorrow, my office between six and seven p.m., and you're ten dollars richer. The only alternative is to phone me."

He sees the wheels turning, I'm thinking that over, so he adds: "Ever get scooped for drunk?"

"It's an occupational hazard."

"If you don't show up or phone, we'll be looking for you. So will street patrol. Your choice. Do I make myself completely clear?"

"Yup."

"Want a ride?"

"Nope."

"The elevator is at the end of the hall. And Bob? You did good. See you tomorrow, please."

"Got a dime for the phone?"

"Sure." He gives me a buck, smiles, and says, "Keep the change."

This is one decent guy.

While I'm walking back to the flop under the viaduct, I'm thinking, *What a fucking nite. Things keep going off around me. Two against one -- very bad odds. I was lucky very lucky. He said please. Please. And he gave me a dollar. That's 4 beers.* The young dick was good, the best I've ever talked to. I could get to like him. Even though he is a cop. I'd trust him to watch my back. He'd trust me to watch his back, too. Only if I was sober, though. There's a TV show for you. The Derelict and the Detective. What a concept.

Back at the flop, I slip into the shadows and listen for anything that doesn't sound right. One has to be alert.

I roll a smoke.

After a few minutes, I quickly hop the retaining wall and start up my trail. Halfway up I stop to pull out two pieces of broom handle, and rig the trip. My security system. Here in the dark, the broom handles will trip anyone coming up the trail. I've got broken glass liberally spread around to cut up any intruders when they fall. Cautious, yes.

There are some scary people out here. People who commit horrifying acts.

My flop is nestled under a concrete flange fluted out over a cement ledge. Home, a roof over my head, is my cardboard deep-freeze box that folds down flat when I'm away. I spotted this hidey-hole when I worked at the warehouse next door. The regular staff used to come up here to eat lunch and do a number, smoke a joint. No one but me realized the potential of the place as a rent-free abode. So on my last day at the job, I set up the other employees. Ratted them out to the foreman; got them fired so I could have the place to myself. Then I was back at casual labor. I'm a lucky guy.

And a heartless bastard.

That was six months ago or more. Now I'm setting up my cardboard tent in the dark. Glug, glug, glug. The cop's pint is almost gone. Decide to leave a solid hit for breakfast. But I get cold sitting there, reviewing the night's adventure. Screw the morning—glug. I've got the pills, and my stash. When the bottles are empty, I break them up nice and sharp and keep maintaining my trail. Now I crawl into the tent-box, flap secured by a string. Snug. Got a real buzz off the vodka. Fucking Bruce boB Lee, I giggle. boB broke the rules of survival. My penalty is cracked knuckles and stitches. I did great, though. I'm a lucky guy.

The piss can is inside. I spark up a smoke. This is just like camping at the Bay. All that's missing is fire—that, and everything else. That whole segment of my life.

I light a candle. Always makes me feel better. Deep drag as I roll my spare pants up to make a pillow. The Bay. Singing around the campfire. Michael, row the boat ashore. Kumbaya, my Lord, kumbaya.

Still have things going off in my head. Sure I won. What could I have done differently? Conclusion: shit happens.

I'm still humming, getting sleepy. I put out the candle and grip the foot-long piece of half-inch galvanized pipe to my chest. A great equalizer, pipe.

The reason I sleep with my head away from the door is to be ready in case I get unexpected company. Ready to greet any unwanted guests appropriately. "Give 'em a pipe dream," I giggle.

As Jimmy Durante would say, good night Mrs. Calabash, wherever you are. I'm still giggling. The muscle kid will look just like Durante, nose-wise, in the morning. It exploded. Felt better than great. Felt righteous. Orgasmic.

Bacchus, you have done your work well. I summon Morpheus to my nest...

Adventures

Anything that suited my purposes, I did. Anything that pertained to the rest of the cosmos, I ignored. The comic genius Red Skeleton perfected the lovable bum character called "Freddy the Freeloader." I was just like that—only not so lovable.

One of my preferred methods of dining was on foot in the grocery department of Woodward's Department Store. The strolling gourmand. I always took a shopping cart along as my cover. First, a trip to the bakery. I'd take a couple of fresh-baked crusty rolls, then move on to the sliced meats, then the mustard, and like this I would build a couple of great sandwiches. I'd eat them as I walked around the food floor. When I was full, I'd ditch the cart and—burp—head off to another adventure.

If you were to write a travel brochure for the part of the city I hung out in, you would start with "Adventures Abound in Vancouver's Skid Row." Then you would go on about the hotel bars. "Each is unique," you'd say. "Each a hell unto itself."

The bars in Vancouver all had different hours of operation. The liquor control board limited them to fourteen hours a day but didn't say which ones. Hence if a bar opened at nine a.m., it closed at eleven p.m. If another opened at eleven a.m., it shut down at one. Once you learned the schedule, you could pretty much find a place to drink all day long.

A real bucket-of-blood hotel was the Sunrise. Even if you sat on the periphery, you couldn't help getting drawn in. The washroom was one of the few places left in North America where you could still get attacked by wild Indians. It opened early, at nine thirty, so it had to close early. That didn't matter. By eleven thirty at night, half the customers were passed out on the tables—or in the washroom.

At quitting time the cops would simply back a paddy wagon up to one of the two exits. Everybody left, but the cops told you which door to use. Those who got door-to-door service to the drunk tank were usually happy for the ride and a place to sleep. The scene made me think of Doctor Mengele as the prisoners arrived at Auschwitz. I tried not to drink at the Sunrise.

That's where my self-esteem vestiges drew the line.

It was a different watering hole where I watched a woman kick a businessman's ass.

The guy was a stranger. He stalked into the bar at eleven in the morning looking like a functioning alcoholic on a twister. Maybe he's had a fight with his wife. He needed a shave. You could tell he'd slept in his rumpled suit. When you're a disciple of Ethyl, you learn to notice the purposeful gait, the planting of one foot in front of the other. His eyes were jumpy nervous, his brow sweaty. He ordered four beers. After they came, he had to wait until the waiter left. Then you could almost see him doing a mantra to get his shit together to pick up the glass.

That was the giveaway. This dude was one of us.

He must have forgotten to save a "cure shot" for the morning. At times like that, it's tough to wait for some place, even the Sunrise, to open. Your life goes into suspended animation. You keep motoring, prowling. You're maybe an hour away from the DTs, an hour away from a seizure.

When I was heading into withdrawal, I often had to use two hands to get the beer to my lips. I was too shaky to write a check, even to sign my name. Once I had to prevail on someone else to loan me the price of six beers to settle me down. After that, I walked into the bank like a Rockefeller.

When you're sick and shaky, you get the beer down in front of you but you're motoring so hard that you can't grab it. You feel people are watching. Then you lurch it toward your mouth so hard that you break the glass.

You think I'm kidding, but one time I cut my tongue on the glass trying to get this "cure drink" down in the morning. So I turned the glass and kept drinking from the other side. Then I could feel the euphoria spreading from my heart out to shoulders. Ethyl's magic spell. After that, no problem. The second beer is a piece of cake.

That's how it was with Mister Rumpled. He downed his first two beers with a passion. Then he set in to consume the next two with a more deliberate slowness. He settled down and actually started to have some fun.

Innocently at first he started hitting on an attractive young woman who was playing pool. She brushed him off. So he started hitting harder and cruder. That's when her girlfriend walked over for a talk.

The girlfriend wore jeans and jet boots, and she carried one of those pointy combs in her back pocket. With it, she combed her short hair back into a ducktail. Her shirt was a man's mackinaw with the sleeves rolled up. I could see some poorly done tattoos, the kind of tattoos men get in jail. Obviously she'd pumped some iron.

We all found out that the woman of Mister Rumpled's desire in fact belonged to her. He had better fucking back off, or else she would personally do him bad harm—really fucking bad harm. Did he fucking understand, completely?

If this gal had taken the time out of her busy life to talk to *me* in the manner she was using with Mr. Rumpled, I would have been gone. Toast. Out of there. I may have been pickled, but I wasn't crazy.

Within ten minutes, though, Rumpled was at it again. The asshole was brain-dead! Bull Dyke came back over to his table. Rumpled was leaning back in his chair. In a flash, she kicked the chair out. Suddenly he was flat—with a jet boot on his throat and the pointed end of a sharp comb jabbing into his left ear. The dyke had him totally in her control.

Lucky for him, the waiters descended. They gave Rumpled the heave-ho out the back door of the tavern. Bull Dyke punctuated the scene with truly scary threats. We never saw him again.

For the kid from the Royal City, that was fast action. Even so, it was just another day on the street. I was pretty relaxed all the time in those days—even during shoot-outs.

Once I was staying in a hotel right on Hastings, just west of Main Street, called The Branditz. I was in the bar nursing a beer, my back pointed safely to the wall. In walked some loony with an M-14 carbine, and he blasted off a few rounds. One of the thirty-caliber slugs pierced the cigarette machine right next to my table. The shell punched a four-inch-diameter dent in the machine; at the center of the dent was a small, perfect hole ringed by an inch of bare metal.

Did I hit the deck? Spill my drink? Silly! I just said, "Far out." And then I tried to boost a pack of cigarettes from the assassinated machine.

I tell this story to illustrate the unreasonable nature of alcoholic reasoning. When the bullets hit the vending machine, boB had a boozy brainstorm—hey, maybe it's broken now. Maybe the next guy who puts coins into the machine will find it paying out free cigarettes like a slot machine. That guy would be a lucky genius. And that lucky genius could be me!

But first I went up to the bar and made a big show out of getting change. That way, it would be easier to get reimbursed. Just in case the cigarette machine had actually been shot dead. In other words, incapable of producing any packages whatsoever. I didn't want to get robbed by the machine I was trying to rob. That's not fair.

Such planning, such devious plans! I got the package of smokes I paid for, no more, no less.

Later, outside, I heard that the police took the guy down in front of the Sunrise. He wasn't killed. Neither was the person for whom he had a bone up his nose. But whether one thing or another happened didn't make a whole lot of difference to me. Basically it was just another night in the liquidarium.

Witnesses to a shooting will often give conflicting answers to the question "How many shots were fired?" I can see why. I can't give you an answer at all, because I just wasn't paying much attention at the time. Four, maybe?

Was it four shots? Yeah, it was four shots. Oswald was the one who fired three. But that was different time. Something to do with a president called Kennedy... The Warren Commission...

"Far out, man."

"Far out" also describes another adventure, one that took place at my viaduct safe flop. Early one Sunday afternoon two young men with long hair, classic hippies, came up the hill carrying a large black plastic garbage bag. As soon as I saw them coming, of course, I grabbed my weapon—the length of half-inch pipe that I always clutched to my chest while I slept. I checked around for my other clubs and cave man weapons. If I was going down, I was going to take a couple of the bastards with me.

The BottleHopper

When I was hiding out at the flop, I always felt like Alexander Selkirk, the real-life inspiration for Robinson Crusoe—an island unto my alien self.

But these hippies looked non-threatening. You go with your gut reaction. You're a student of the streets. Guys who smoke pot are really docile. It's the shaved heads and tattoos that you've got to worry about. So I decided to announce my presence—I didn't want them to panic.

"Hey, man. Any heat around?" they asked.

"Nope."

"Can we do-up fifteen lids?" they asked. They had just scored a kilo of pot and were looking for a safe place to divide it into roughly one-ounce bags. But first they wanted to clean it—that is, remove the stems and seeds by rubbing the herb vigorously between their hands.

"Sure, no problem. Glad to have some company."

We smoked a couple of joints, and, to be hospitable, I retrieved a bottle of wine from my larder. We had a great time drinking wine, smoking pot, and cleaning and bagging the pot. They left me all the stems, which I used later to make some great tea. And then, when—alas, too soon—they finished, they gave me a generous amount of pot and several rolled joints. I cleaned up the seeds, and put them in a large jar. I sparked up another joint. I was stoned!

Far out!

The munchies struck like a hammer. I was ravenous. I sortied to a grocery store for hot dogs and buns. I always used to steal those little plastic packages of mustard and ketchup from fast-food places, so I already had the condiments.

Then, to cook the tube steaks, I needed fire.

I was pretty well wasted and never one to do things in half-measures. I dragged six wooden pallets up the hill. These were big, square oil-soaked pallets three feet across. Enough fuel for a funeral pyre. The flames soared up ten feet high and then, unknown to me, started curling under the bridge deck. The smoke was causing traffic jams on the viaduct above. Meanwhile I was pigging out. Oblivious!

Afterwards I peed on the fire in a worthless attempt to douse the flames. Hell, I couldn't get even close because of the heat. Then I crawled into my cardboard tent. It was just like camping out at the Bay—fire and everything. I fantasized about being Bobby Potseed the following spring. Planting my seeds. Turning on the whole city! Then I passed into a deep sleep. Dreaming of a blue ox; couldn't figure where he fit into the Johnny Appleseed story.

The next thing I knew, half the Vancouver fire department was there. I was hosed out of the sanctuary of my cardboard tent.

I think well on my feet, even when soaked and stoned, even in circumstances like these. I spun a believable story about some other guys lighting the fire. I said that I was just waiting around till tomorrow, when I could pick up a check and then get back to work. The police took me to Catholic Charities for the night.

I had a shower and was gone with first light.

I avoided the pad for a few days, except for late at night when a visit to my larder was necessary. No more fires, though. Even boB learned from his mistakes.

My supply of pot was well stashed; one never knows when one will need the calming effect of a joint. Pot really helped if I had no booze. If I was coming down, it really took the edge off things.

Life on the skids certainly had its edges.

When you're out on the street, life seems to pulse with an undercurrent of impending disaster. Something is always going down. Always some action happening. Easy to observe if you train yourself to look for it. Dope scores—real dope, the needle variety. Cocaine—sometimes an eightball, usually less. A bundle of heroin stored in a balloon. Clothing still warm from being boosted. Bizarre sexual encounters being negotiated. Lots of interesting stuff.

You have to keep tough. If you get sick, you can't work. If you're out of work, you're out of booze. No booze and you're in withdrawal. Not a good place for me to be.

But that's where I was one Sunday when I managed to scrounge the price of a large bottle of vanilla, the sixteen-ounce size. The proprietor of a grocery store knew I was sick, and still he deliberately sold me a bottle of the synthetic stuff. I proceeded to a back alley and put down a couple of shots. Yuk! Then I made my way to the park to kill some time.

Victory Square, colloquially called Pigeon Park, was a place to hang out on a Sunday and score free glugs of booze. Once I passed out on the grass there and when I woke up discovered that I'd pissed myself. I had to wait until I dried out. I wasn't going to walk around wet. My self-esteem vestiges drew the line there, too. Even there at the park, standing in a group of men passing around a bottle of rubby, I'd have moments of clarity. Once I seemed to wake up and notice the faces of the men around me. I saw the broken, twisted noses that had been flattened by sucker-punches, the heavy, scarred-up eyebrows damaged by too many head-butts—typical features of the chronic. But these guys also had facial scabs and open sores around their mouths. And here we were, all sucking from the same bottle of poison. Suddenly, I just felt like shit.

Maybe the rubbing alcohol worked as a disinfectant.

Anyway, I was down at the park that day wondering why the vanilla hadn't worked its magic. I ran into a crony from casual labor who was also sick. I offered him a drink of my prize, but he turned it down.

"That's the fake stuff," he said. "The natural stuff is the only kind that has alcohol in it. You got ripped off."

I went ballistic. I stalked back to the corner grocery store dangerously angry, fully prepared to hurt the Oriental storekeeper if necessary. He read my mood correctly and gave me three bottles of the natural vanilla, all the big sixteen-ounce size. For free. I left the store placated, and felt justified in scaring the man half to death.

Then a little buzzer went off in my head. Beware of Orientals giving gifts. I was sure the bastard had called the police. I had to disappear fast. I don't blame the guy. I was sick and therefore scary to him. I was motoring down an alley and saw one of those large metal dumpsters, opened the hatch, and jumped in. Drank half a bottle of the stuff. While waiting for it to do its calming magic, I rolled a cigarette.

Halfway through the second bottle of vanilla I was starting to believe that the dumpster was actually a Sherman tank participating in Operation Overlord. The invasion of occupied Europe. Was I on Sword, Juno, or Gold Beach? Hell, I was on all three! Killing Huns! For home, for country, apple pie, natural vanilla, and the God-given right to live democratically free in a dumpster.

Had to be really careful inside these things, especially with the smoking. Some poor bastard ended up falling asleep while smoking in a dumpster, and he torched himself. The prize dumpsters were those that the Sally Anne and Goodwill put out to receive used clothing. In the winter you could burrow into the clothing and stay warm.

I waited until the small hours of the morning before leaving my imaginary tank. I had to score some work Monday or I'd be in detox, or the hospital...or worse.

Casual labor was my salvation, my only means of income. The casual labor office enabled me to last as long as I did on the street. Sometimes the work would turn out to be an actual semi-permanent job. I'd stay with the job until I'd accumulated a couple of hundred dollars. Then I'd draw out all my pay and phone in sick, saying I had diarrhea or whatever.

Until I'd earned enough residual money to quit, I took a daily draw of ten dollars. That's what I needed to survive. The price of a fifth of vodka in those days was eight dollars and sixty-three cents. That left some change for a store-bought sandwich and a few beers. Perhaps I needed two bits for bus fare. If I was hungry, the Sally, Catholic Charities, Central City Mission, and several other places gave out free food. The burning question that I often asked was "Why spoil a good drunk by eating?"

My skin crawls as I journey and slog through these years in my memory. I think of body lice, fleas, wine sores, scabies—scabies were the worst—and I feel revulsion; palpable, real, and disgusting.

The rat is the king of filth. Because Vancouver is a seaport, huge Norwegian rats infest the waterfront and its warehouses. I once had a job working in the warehouse that supplied Lipton dehydrated soup for all of Vancouver. Each individual portion of soup came in a metal package. The rats had learned to eat through the outer cardboard boxes and then gnaw through the metal package to find the soup.

Our job was to help the permanent staff do inventory. We had to move out a lot of stock that had become buried behind some newer inventory. So we formed a conveyor belt of men and passed out the boxes of older stock. We were working from the top of the stockpile, so essentially we were creating a large vacant hole, a pit that kept descending into the newer soup-boxes.

Suddenly there was a shout. The two men who were working down in the hole scampered out as though they'd caught on fire. We all looked down into the pit—it was about eight feet deep— and stared at the rat they'd discovered. The thing had its head in a soup box, and it seemed to be acting according to the ostrich theory: if your head is hidden, you are therefore invisible. But its entire torso was visible, and it was huge.

One of the regulars went and got the resident cat. We sat around the pit waiting for the cat to be thrown in. I felt like a Roman at the Coliseum. Down she went. For a few seconds the big feline seemed confused, unsure why it had been tossed in the hole. Then she discovered it—the rat! She gave a primal scream and attacked. The cat did a killing bite to the neck, just as its distant African cousins do, and the drama was over.

So was our work for the day. No one would go back into the hole. We loaded up our pockets to overflowing with soup packages and left.

I could go on and on with these stories and give them more significance than they deserve. The point? The point is that, unlike the rat, I survived.

I learned to give a phony name when scooped for drunk. If you got scooped three times in a month, the government sent you to a mandatory dry-out of thirty days at Alouette River Institute. A bloody jail. Not my idea of fun, so I chucked my ID. The only time this was a problem was when I woke up in the tank and couldn't remember what name I had given. This stupidity once cost me two extra hours in the drunk tank while I sat there trying to recall the name "Fred Farkle" from the TV show *Laugh in.*

Another time, two of us were walk-in scoops. More like a couple of fruit loops. We were looking for the other guy's squeeze, who maybe had some money. Often Anita would turn a trick or two for drinking money. So we went into the cop-shop to see if they'd scooped Anita for hooking. I guess coming in from the cold night into the heat of the police station put us over the top. The pint we shared in the alley on the way to the station also might have helped. While we were in the police station, I went to the shitter and drank half of another pint. I left the rest of that pint stashed behind the toilet for Joe to find. By the time that pint was gone, we were pretty far gone ourselves.

We didn't find Anita, but they kept us for being drunk.

Another time I got scooped twice in one day. A personal record! They picked me up the first time around one in the morning on my way to the flop. I was released around eight-thirty—and then I only had an hour to kill before the bar at the Savoy Hotel opened.

At the Savoy I nursed a few beers until ten-thirty, when the liquor store opened. I purchased a bottle of Thunderbird wine and went around the back alley to consume it. I took a couple of good hits and then had to pee. When the black and white police cruiser came around the corner, there I was in all my glory— with my dick in one hand having a leak, and a bottle in the other guzzling down the wine.

What a loser!

They didn't put me in the back seat until I finished my pee and the bottle. It was a short ride, around the block. Another six hours of the tank. Another phony name. And the beat went on and on...

Enough of this stuff!

School Days

Ring, ring goes the bell. Bottlehopper wakes up feeling like hell. Slowly coming to in a one-room flop—a lousy excuse for a cheap hotel.

Actually, I'm pretty flush. I have a wind-up alarm clock. I scored a real good job on a construction site. They know I've got a booze problem, but they put up with it because they like me and I'm a good worker. Tomorrow is Friday, and my flop is paid up until the next Friday.

I sure am sick, though.

Got a really bad cold. I feel cold. Not eating. Coughing up lots of phlegm—which is okay. The clear phlegm is okay. It's that other phlegm I've got to watch for, the yellow and green kind. Green and yellow. Those aren't man-made colors. Those are the colors of mold and rotting leaves and compost and life returning to the slime from which it arose. Yellow and green mean bronchitis or worse—pneumonia. I'm weak and shivering with a racking cough.

Wish the room had a window. Wish it was warmer. No question, I have to work today. But first I have to drag myself out of bed. That's work. That may be all the work I can do. Open the door, walk to the end of the hall, and check the weather through the window.

Sleet.

It's a real raw, murderous, gray morning full of an all-day mean looking sky.

I have to get some food into me or the wine sores on my legs are going to turn septic. Three of them, dime-sized. I have to do the Doctor boB cleaning. It always smarts. Wine sores are like bed sores, they don't heal. boB is anemic.

Safely back in the room, I remove my pants and begin. I have found that the best home treatment is to pick the scabs right off. Encourage the sore to bleed a little. Then I get the old standby, Aqua Velva after-shave, and pour it into the sores. Shit, they hurt like hell. Then dab them dry with toilet paper and cover them with clean band aids that I secreted from the first-aid kit at work. Of course this hurts. That's the way Vince Lombardi would have wanted it—I can play hurt.

Big deal!

Dump the rest of the after-shave in a cup, add water, prost. Down the hatch. Wasn't all that bad. I just didn't breathe for a second or two. No big deal.

I'll do four swallows of vodka before work. Two now, glug, glug. Racking cough. Swallow a bunch; don't puke—I need my medicine. Keep the stuff down. Gag, swallow. Bite the bullet. God, that's corny.

Take the pain; that's what it means. I'm the one who wanted to play alcoholic. It's my life; I made the choice. If I keep the next two down and then leave immediately for work, I'll be okay until noon.

My plan is to try to get to work. Tell the foreman how sick I am and that I need a cash advance of one hundred dollars. Tell him that I'm going to the doctor this afternoon, get some medicine. Then rest all weekend. Be back Monday ready to rumble.

I'm still shivering.

Washed my socks in the sink last night, so as usual I'm putting them on damp. They'll warm up in a few minutes. Then the liquor store, antibiotic powder from the drug store, perhaps I will go see a doctor. I'll get some canned soup for sure, warm it on the radiator or in hot water from the sink. Small pleasures.

I'm shivering so much that I get back under the covers. Try to shift my mind into neutral and let it coast to a stop.

As my dear old mother used to say, if you make your bed you sleep in it. I'll be okay once I get moving. Got to push. No choice now; couldn't make it through the weekend without a major re-supply of booze. It's my plan: so it is written, so it shall be.

Still ten minutes before the walk to the bus. Might as well stay warm till the last minute. I'm probably not in that bad a shape, except for my health.

They owe me for all last week, three full days this week, half a day today. I still have gloves, hat, warm coat, boots. I even have some pills, some Librium twenty-fives—capsules, green at one end, white at the other. I'm learning all about pharmaceuticals, while mixing them with ethyl and methyl alcohol. My philoso-phy with pills: if one is good, two's twice as good, and the square root of 4 is 2.

Here are some interesting recipes for oblivion: Mix Librium or Valium with a fifth of cheap wine, and get eight hours of oblivion. Mix one large bottle of codeine cough syrup with a bottle of Scope mouthwash—oblivion for six hours, usually with a par-tial blackout. Substitute natural vanilla for the alcohol in any of the above recipes.

I'm a lucky guy, sure. A friend gave me these Librium. Correc-tion: an *acquaintance* gave them to me. Got no friends.

Screw the bullshit. If I don't make it today, I'll be in detox or worse.

Life deals a lemon. How do you make lemonade? I never learned. The fact that I can't do lemonade has brought me many times within a pubic hair of death. Once boB even hacked up his wrists in a feeble attempt to exacerbate the end. Alas, boB had no balls. He knew the right way to do it—the femoral artery or the carotid. That would give the desired result. Do that, and it's "Good-by, Fluffy."

Good-by, Fluffy. That low-culture witticism comes from the Dick-and-Jane readers we used in elementary school. You remem-ber: Spot was the dog, Puff was the kitten, and Fluffy the cat.

Still five minutes to go. Christ, it's like "The Day The Earth Stood Still." I listen to the clock to make sure it's still running. Wind it up. Start thinking of somewhere warm, anywhere. Ha-waii. I went there in 1966, for my honeymoon. Puerto Vallarta, Mazatlan, Grand Cayman. Would they be warm enough? It's tough right now even to remember the names of warm places. How about Hell. Would Hell be warm enough?

I finish rolling a smoke, spark it up, take a deep drag. Then that racking cough again. I run the water and spit it down the sink. Now a philosophical consideration: It takes three things to make a smoke—tobacco, rolling papers, and matches. If you could only have one, which one would it be? Think about it. You can find tobacco anywhere. Butts galore on the street. All you have to do is patrol the gutters before the street sweeper makes the scene. And matches—not a problem. Even a guy in a suit will give you a light. Even if he's disgusted, he'll go that far. It doesn't cost him anything.

Papers are the key.

It's time. Boots on. Vodka, as scheduled. Glug, glug. I'm salivating—keep swallowing, stupid. That's better. Salivation is a Pavlovian response, a conditioned reflex. Get moving quick, grab your jacket, and padlock the door.

While I'm walking to the bus stop, I keep thinking about a hot bath with soap. Lots of soap. God, this is getting tougher. Picking up butts on the way. Even though I've got tobacco in my pouch, I still do it—strip off the paper, dump it in. Another adaptation to the environment.

The other day I got sucker-punched just asking a guy for a smoke. I didn't read him right. Didn't ask him right. Let my guard down, seemed needy, felt needy. I made myself a target. BANG, like a strike of lightning right in the face. I went back on my ass, bleeding from the nose. My own fault. If you act like prey, you will be prey. You just can't walk around with a "Kick Me" sign taped on your face.

Probably his old man was an alcoholic. Who knows.

Then the worst part. No damage done—the guy helps me up. Mumbles he's sorry. Gives me five bucks and the rest of his package of tailor-made smokes. Pities the pitiful. Blessed is he who comforts the afflicted and all that shit.

Hey, five bucks is five bucks. That equates to a pint of vodka (three dollars and sixty-three cents) and several beers. All it costs is five bucks—that, and letting somebody smack you.

You've come a long way, boB. A couple of years ago you would have ripped his fucking lips off and fined him all the cash he was packing for having made you go through the exercise. That was then—the old, gone time.

I shuffle onto the bus cold and trembling. Get a few looks. Nothing serious, same old same old. But I'm remembering the guy back in the Savoy, the one who, like Dillinger, wasn't going to be taken alive. I'm turning into a pussy. Hardly think about conventional sex anymore, sex with a woman. Just pull it. It's clean, no commitment, no diseases, no missed periods, I don't have to depend on anyone. Almost there. Next stop. Pull the cord.

God I'm cold. "Suck it in, asshole. One foot in front of the other. Push. Stretch the envelope." Remember: predators survive.

It's raw out here. Wet, cold rain and sleet, shivering, and the cough making me convulse in spasms. I spit up a huge gob and tell it, "Get out and walk!" This day is so raw that if it were meat, Doctor Frankenstein could bring it back to life.

Joe, the foreman, breaks the silence.

"Bob, you look like shit."

Joe, I feel like shit!

"Bad cold. Feeling rotten. Going to suggest I work till noon, then head over to the clinic, get some antibiotics. Have to get an advance, say a hundred bucks. Then I'll rest up tomorrow and the weekend."

"Sounds like a good idea, Bob. I'll see Bill and get the money. We'll pay you for four hours today; don't worry about doing anything. I'll be right back."

These are nice people.

Might as well do a little work till he gets back. Keep myself warm. Better take the Librium so I can make it till noon.

And so I do. But I don't make it till noon. The farthest I get is to the dumpster with a load of scrap wood. Really coughing. Can't stop coughing. Oh shit.

Dizzy. Feel like I'm falling. Can't stop coughing. Difficulty breathing...

Good-by, Fluffy.

Zapped

Just silence. No light. Nothing to feel. Just privacy and peace. God, what a lovely calm! No sleeping with one eye open. No broken glass to cut, no pipe to maim, no imagined visitors, no demons.

No guilt.

I'm floating. My body is cool, physically cool, but it's a calming cool, a coolness that's away, far away.

ZAP.

With an instant, crackling surge every muscle in my body turns to steel. Fingers, toes, arms, legs jolt out, out, out. Tighter. Anguish.

My chest heaves. I suck in gallons of air. What the hell was that? Relax! Think! Don't open your eyes. Cough, choking, gag, spit, swallow. I'm having a seizure, perhaps that's it. I liked it better where I was.

I breathe slowly again, shallower—that's it, now I'm getting back there. Peace! What a feeling, what a great feeling, floating on water, no cares, almost narcotic, truly euphoric. Calm waters, still waters, caressing waters, I'm there.

ZAPPP.

There it is again! My whole body exploding. I caught air that time. Lifted me right off the bed. Can't move. Paralyzed? I flop like a fish, but my arms and legs can't work. Fighting. I'm buried in sawdust again. Can that be? Can that happen again? Buried alive again?

Then I get it—the smell. The medical stench of solvents and sterilizers. I'm in restraint. Shit, it must be the hospital. I get it. Electricity. Zap zap zap. They're putting those electric paddles on me. Heart attack? Am I dying? Again?

I'm seeing spots. No, a spotlight. Bright blinding light. Someone's shining a fucking light in here! Get out! Get out. Struggling, but I can't. Voices muffled muddled mixed-up. Then one voice as though it's right in my face:

"Bob, you are safe. You are in a hospital."

It's a doctor. You can always tell the voice of a doctor. It's got confidence. The kind of confidence that knows, unlike you, that he gets to go home after the shift.

"Bob, open your eyes."

"No!"

Alcoholic reasoning. I am a contrary. OUCH! The fucker pinches me, right where the shoulder hits the neck. Playing hardball. With me! Bloody restraints. Let me at the prick!

"Stay with me, Bob. Pay attention. Stay with me! Open your eyes."

The prick pinches me again! This dude means business. Okay, okay, give me a minute! I always did respect authority. That's how I was screwed up as a child.

WOW!

The lights are wild. Supernova bright. I blink my eyes a few times. It's like a strobe light. Like a hit of blotter acid, but no color. Only blinding light. Cool. Magic mushrooms? Light bright and noise mumbled, jumbled sounds like a video game. Electronic beeping sounds.

Something down my throat. A long piece of spaghetti, maybe. Feels like they're pulling it out. And now a mask. They're putting on a mask. Phantom of the Opera. Knock it off. The fucking thing's hissing. Hey, they put a fucking snake down my throat!

I'm motoring. I'm gone. Let me out of here!

Can't. Restrained. Struggling.

A female voice is fairy-godmothering me: "It's only an oxygen mask, Bob. Please listen. Breathe steadily. Nothing is going to hurt you."

Okay. I always was a sucker for skirts. Always followed my little head. Definitely a boy thing.

I am coherent. I'm definitely here now. Reality is an emergency ward. That other place, wherever it was, is gone. Kind faces, female, smiling. I try to say thank you but it comes out:

"Croak you."

Gently my head is lifted, and an angel who looks like a woman with intense blue eyes gives me some water. It is the coolest, the purest, the soothingest water I have ever tasted. I try again; this time it works.

"Thank you."

I'm still cold, *only* now it's *real* cold, physical cold. Shivering. I want to say something about my discomfort, but I don't. It's not that I'm macho. I just don't like assholes who cry in their beer. You do the crime, you do the time. Bite the bullet, big boB. You chose *this.*

Then it hits me with a spasm of disgust. I chose this? I chose this? I'm the biggest goddamn liar in the world.

I can't stop drinking. I can't stop drinking to save my life. I only weigh a hundred and fifty pounds. Christ, when I was born I think I weighed a hundred and forty. My normal weight is close to two hundred. The body is breaking down, boB. You are not a predator anymore, sport. You're barely surviving.

I start noticing things. Drips in both arms and one leg. The red one—bet that's blood. How astute of you, Holmes. Now they're putting more blankets on me, and I'm starting to slow down on the shivering. I start taking inventory the best I can, being strapped down and all. As near as I can tell, I still have all the feeling in my body. Nothing seems to be broken. I do not feel pain. Just the shivery cold, and the coughing.

Can't ask anyone.

That's against my personal code of omerta. If somebody wants to tell me something, let them tell me. Otherwise, I honestly can't remember. Can't remember getting here. I remember cold, wind, shivering, cold sleet, cold hands, coughing, cold feet, construction site. Been weak for days. Bad cold. Coughing big-time at the flop; *lots* of phlegm, clear and productive. Went to work. Coughing, coughing. That's it. I'm coughing now, for real, here in this place. Kidney tray polished silver held up by hands, hands with no face. I spit out the phlegm. Yuk! That totally exhausted me; I'm actually seeing spots. If I was standing I bet I'd have hit the deck. I would have passed out for sure.

The phlegm is no longer "clear and productive." Shit!

I am in trouble.

Pneumonia—the p is silent, just like the pee in swimming. Where did that come from, that little witticism? From the "before" time, from the good time, the gone time. Get a grip, asshole. We are in the here-and-now. Zooming again. When canary howls, Pluto is in line with Donald Duck... Zooz.

Some time must have gone by. I'm really disoriented. "Just must have passed out at the job," I guess.

Chest is heavy, tight. Bronchitis for sure. Probably pneumonia. Can't remember getting a ride to X-ray. That'll come next. Two drips and blood. While I was out they must have sampled my blood, found my count down, probably anemic. Haven't been eating right lately. Haven't been eating at all for a few days.

The body's giving out. I gave it my best shot. Now I need help, care. I'm done like dinner. Put me in a nuthouse, hand me the pen, I'll sign up for a lobotomy.

There's a leprechaun standing at the foot of my bed. Great! Not on the floor, on the bed. Rude little fuck, on the bed with his funny shoes on. I'll teach him some manners.

Can't move still in restraints.

He's wearing a green and black outfit. Funny hat, bushy red hair, freckles, blue eyes, and one of those strip-like beards that seems to surround his face. Funny shoes like black loafers with big silver buckles. The hat has a buckle on it, too. The look of the devil in his eyes. Cool little dude.

Perhaps if I ignore him he will go away.

He's not a problem, though. I've seen him before in detox. He only looks at me; never speaks. I've tried talking to him, but he doesn't respond. He's harmless; therefore, he's quite unreal. I only see him when I am in withdrawal.

The room has gone quiet. No one around now. I guess the worst part's over. Here I am, just hanging loose. Hanging loose with my mute little Irish pal. Shit, bugger, poop, damn. I'm a mess. No vestiges. No nothing. The not-unpleasant sound of the oxygen mask hisses and gurgles in the background. I try to remain still. Mind over matter.

A calm descends over the scene until the doctor's presence breaks in.

"Bob," he says, and I jump what feels like two feet into the air. Still in restraints, but I certainly get some air. The old eyes were closed. Doctor got me by surprise. Nerves are shot, too. I'd say I'm pretty much a mess.

"You look a lot better. Had us really worried there."

The doctor is a gaunt, kind-looking man with deep brown eyes. He's smiling at me. That confidence in his voice—familiarity, perhaps?

"Sorry, doctor. What happened?"

"What do you remember?"

"Not much. Coughing and cold, mostly. Suppose I passed out."

"We got you by ambulance about three hours ago. From a construction site. Respiration was slow and labored, cyanotic. We pulled blood samples, did a blood gasses sample, too. You had a lot of carbon dioxide in your blood. Have you been taking any pills with the booze?"

"I had about four ounces of vodka before work this morning, and I took six or eight Librium."

"Well, Bob, that helps. Thanks for your honesty. And it matches the symptoms. You stopped breathing. It was a combination of the tranquilizers and the booze, your lung function, malnutrition, and the fact that your red blood count is down. What's happening with you is that the alcohol and pills, because they're both depressants, are taking you into a condition so deep that only your vital functions are still going. The sympathetic nervous system. If you start coughing, you could choke to death because you're unaware of the parasympathetic functions of the central nervous system."

"You're using pretty big words, doctor."

"That's only because I know you, Bob. You've been here before. I know about your intelligence. The sores on your leg, by the way. You have those telltale red lines starting. Do you know what that's about?"

"Blood poisoning, doctor. The red lines are in the lymphatic system. They would be heading towards the groin, to the lymph nodes. Can't figure. I flushed them with Aqua Velva after-shave and drank the rest."

Zooz.

Then I'm gone. Trapped in my head—alone, not working, not drinking. I start thinking about blood. Arterial blood, venous blood, blood pumped by the heart. Four chambers, two atriums, two ventricles—tricuspid, bicuspid valves. Positive and negative blood grouping. The Rh factor. The rhesus monkey. Prehensile tail—old world. Chimps and gorillas—new world. Platelets. Hemoglobin. Oxygenated blood. Erythrocytes—red blood cells. Leukocytes—white blood cells. The lymphatic system. Spanish aristocracy. Russian, too. Hemophilia. Anastasia's dead. Anesthesia. You heard it here first.

Zooz.

The doctor's calm voice brings me back. "I have admitted you. We have to get some work done on you. You almost died. We're sending you up for chest X-rays. You're full of fluid, Bob, and we're afraid you have pneumonia. We've started antibiotics."

I giggle. Not at the doctor. At my Irish friend on his shoulder. I explain my behavior. I make sure that the doctor knows that I know that the leprechaun isn't real and that he's quite harmless.

"The little shit's doing a jig on your shoulder."

When he hears that, the leprechaun sticks out his tongue, makes faces, then turns around, drops his pants, and moons me. I laugh, and the doctor smiles a kind of glad-you're-back smile.

"Can we take you out of restraints now? Will you be okay?"

"Yes. But leave the roll-bars up, please. In case I have a seizure."

"For goodness' sake, talk to us, Bob. Let us know what you need."

"Dilantin. For the seizures. The rest I can handle."

"I was really fearful, this time, Bob. You're getting worse."

I think to myself: *Stop buttering me up, Doc. Give it to me straight.* But the joke is too stupid to say out loud. I know how I am. Sick and weary.

They kept me in the hospital just over three weeks. I did have pneumonia. Then alcohol-abuse counselors came to interview me, and they sent me to a place called Fraser House. It's a halfway house in Mission, just an hour from Vancouver—a place for rehabilitation and work.

If there was a "bottom" to my slide through skid row, I guess this was it. I wish it was that simple. The hell of it is, the recovery from the disease is just as progressive as the descent into it. After this kick at the can, I got eighteen months sober. I wish I could say straight, too, but I used a lot of pot during that 18 months—to "take the edge off." Sure, Bob. I did make some big steps forward. But I took a few back.

The road to recovery is fraught with danger and setbacks. But so what? Whether or not he deserved it, the real Bob was getting another shot at life. This little voice in my head kept saying, "Bob, this may be your only salvation. Don't mess it up."

Surely I was sick and tired of being sick. But I was also honest enough to realize that I was now powerless, that I couldn't stop on my own. I couldn't bear the pain of being sober. Whenever I got sober, I saw that my life was a terrible mess. How could I possibly begin coping with that mess without the phony fortification of Ethyl Alcohol?

This state called "sobriety"—could I even achieve it, much less maintain it?

Fraser House

A counselor from Fraser House picked me up at the hospital. He was driving a white Econoline van. He took me to the detoxification center in the heart of skid row, and from there we made our trip out to Mission.

The rehabilitation counselors at the hospital had told me about Fraser House—a stately old residential home located in a small town. The provincial government had converted the place into a live-in, work-oriented, rehabilitation center for recovering alcoholics. The facility housed fifteen recovering alcoholics for the duration of the eight-week course.

In the van I kept wondering: *Good grief, why am I so edgy.*

Because you're scared, boB, was my silent response. *Scared of this challenge, scared of change, afraid of failure.*

It's contrary to my nature to second-guess myself. Hell-bent Bob is a kinetic-energy guy, a "when you're in doubt, do something" type. But now he had some crippling doubts. How long had it been since he was up there in the frontal lobe, riding along with boB and Ethyl A? Since forever, I thought.

In fact, this was the first time in years that I'd been sober for two whole weeks. Of course, I'd had no choice—no pubs in the hospital, and the doctor wouldn't let me out. He knew I'd go straight to a bar. We both knew the reality of my addiction—always the need pulling at me, the thirst. If I walked down a hallway and smelled methyl alcohol—rubby—I'd get a hard on. The knowledge that I can escape the Zooz when I'm numb. Escape reality when I'm drinking.

At detox we picked up two men. While we were there, a third guy showed up. His wife dropped him off. She was driving in the family station wagon. Taking Daddy downtown to detox.

I could see him through the window—a tall, robust guy with well-groomed, curly hair and a how-the-hell-are-you handshake. This was my first sight of Douglas. The three strangers climbed into van, talking loudly. I just slumped in the corner, using my listening skills.

Douglas was a businessman. He had sparkling gray eyes and a quick wit. He was smarter than your average drunk. To me that meant that he was still functioning with his alcoholism. Time would tell. But I knew that he was good people—a decent guy. One indicator: his employer was paying his full wages while he attended the course.

There was also a Celtic bricklayer, Jimmy, a real rounder with the most captivating sing-song Irish brogue I've ever heard. Jimmy showed some wear; he bore a few nasty scars and a nose significantly left of bilateral symmetry. He embodied the stereotype of the volatile Irishman—a grand soul who would knock you on your ass for not agreeing with him, then help you up with tears in his eyes.

Stan, the third alcoholic, drove a tour bus, serving destinations like Reno and Vegas. Tall and good looking with salt-and-pepper gray hair, Stan made it clear from the get-go that he was a pussy hound. He suggested that we pick up some company if we passed any ladies hitchhiking. He also said that his wife had given him the ultimatum—straighten up with the booze and stop chasing skirts or get out.

Jimmy was fifty-one. Douglas and Stan were in their early forties. I was the youngest at thirty-six. Believe it when I say that I looked the oldest—white-gray hair and a slouched-over walk. My alcoholic reasoning prevented me from doing much interacting. Barriers, defensive shields, and general doubts about everyone and everything were firmly in place. I was still cautious, still in the street mode of survival, using hard-earned skills. I was comfortable saying little.

But when Stan suggested that we take up a collection and stop for a couple of dozen beers, I lost it and laughed. Douglas kept offering me cigarettes. After the first one, I politely declined. (I was brought up properly.) But he kept shaking his pack at me, so I took another one on the condition that he'd let me teach him how to roll his own. That was a mistake. Douglas was manually spastic. Over the next six weeks we were all going to share many laughs over his clumsiness. We bonded at his expense.

Despite his lack of manual dexterity, Douglas was cool. Like me, he chuckled and participated in the banter, but he didn't really open up. Not like the other two—the bus-driver and the bricklayer, Mutt and Jeff. Like me, Douglas knew how easy it is to participate in conversation without revealing anything about yourself and your feelings. I attributed this to my habit of living in survival mode. I couldn't tell what Douglas attributed it to, since he had arrived in the family station wagon. But I took his reserve as a sign of his intelligence. I was hoping he played bridge.

I joined in tentatively. The truth is, we were all being tentative. The conversation was a little forced and a lot louder than necessary. We were all acting like kids going off to summer camp, trying to sound brave by being loud. These guys were up-tight-assed, just like me. I took that as a good sign. In fact, I'm sure I had an intuition of what was to be—that over the next few months we were going to bond like the Three Musketeers.

There were four of us, too—just as in *the Three Musketeers*. Why there are four musketeers when the title clearly specifies "three," I really can't say. As everybody knows, the fourth one is D'Artagnan. Even though he shows up late, he does happen to be the whole point of the story. And he's at least as good a Musketeer as the rest of them. So I say the math is wrong. And therefore it's damned ironic that the author's name is pronounced "Dum-ass."

Riding the bus to rehab is the perfect time to think about shit like that.

"Let's have a song, boys," Jimmy said. "It will be makin' us to feel better. Do you Canadian heathens know anything of the Irish and their songs?"

He then slipped into a clear tenor and began singing "A Wild Colonial Boy." We all joined in and sang with our eyes looking far away, lost in our thoughts. As I look back sober through the kaleidoscope of past events, this moment always causes me pain. These were real men, good men, with an illness. At the moment, though, "A Wild Colonial Boy" made us happy. We sang our way to Fraser House, and upon our arrival we met our counselors and signed up for the course.

It was an intensive total immersion course. Fraser House took only fifteen men at a time, and eleven men were already in residence. Some of them went outside every day to work their day jobs; they had finished the course. Others were waiting for the course to begin.

It was fortunate that I had learned how to walk quietly and carry an imaginary stick. Some of these dudes were quite mentally ill. Out on the streets, I only lowered my standards and hung out with pukes like these if they had booze to share. Here I had no choice. Not that I myself was much of a prize—a physical wreck, an emotional mess, and a long-time resident of the land of denial. I had three regular addresses in that never-never land: "Poor Me," "Why Me," and "I'm Mad As Hell." But the hell of it was that some of these dudes even scared a veteran street-survivor like me.

Jimmy and Stan were able to take care of themselves. Jimmy was fearless; Stan was big. Of the four of us, I was by far the scariest. I had nothing left to lose. I would hurt you without hesitation because basically, deep down, I was mean. I still am mean, I'm sorry to say. At least sober I can control my anger.

The three of us all decided to keep an eye out for Douglas. Physically he was big enough, but he lacked survival skills. With us, he earned his bones by being kind. But the trait of kindness does not provide an evolutionary advantage when you're living among rounders and sick drunks. We protected him. We shared a nonverbal understanding that if you fucked with one of us, you fucked with us all. After all, there is an *esprit de corps* that exists between alcoholics. We all know about being sick and needing a drink to straighten out, or about needing the entrance fee to a bar.

It seems strange to relive these times.

Douglas and I grew closer as we vented some of our honest feelings. My own story was just too bizarre for him. I knew that he doubted me at first. He told me later that he checked me out with some contacts in the lumber industry. Many of his contacts knew my father and, indirectly, me.

The fact that he checked me out was good, because afterwards he never doubted my veracity. But I couldn't understand why he didn't believe me right from the start. Good grief. Why would I lie about being such a complete failure? Failure as a husband, failure as a father—failure as a hero at Birch Bay.

During the first few days of the course we ran the gamut of emotions. Long-dormant interpersonal skills had to be re-learned. We were all trying to cut each other some slack despite an atmosphere of frustration, loud noises, and the idiosyncrasies of personalities. It was a real powder-keg environment. The first week, three guys were given the boot for fighting. Douglas was in awe, almost disbelief, over some of the stories and sick adventures that the rest of us unveiled. He was a bit naive—the way I had been, once, long ago.

Things could get sweaty tense in the group sessions. The counselor would stay silent and let the group interact. If someone thought you were pulling the old bullshit, he would call your bluff. Of course, he was supposed to do this with care and concern. Yeah, sure thing. Usually the one calling your bluff was neither caring nor concerned. Just sick of your bullshit.

One day someone said: "The God-damned Catholics are ruining Ireland." It was a remark tailor-made for Jimmy, and it jolted his Gaelic soul like an overcharged cattle prod. He had dark black eyes, and when he was angry they took on a sinister glow. Not even I would talk to him about religion or the politics of Belfast. No matter how you approached the subject, Jimmy had a knack for bringing matters to a head—and he used that knack now as he replied in a menacing, measured tone, "Just what do you suppose gives a Protestant bastard such as you, in this room with me, the right to question the authority of the Mother Church—you heathen Orange bastard mother fucker!"

Suddenly, fists were ready to fly. Fortunately, the counselor jumped in and defused the situation. It would have been fun to see Jimmy in action, but it would have cost the Irishman the remainder of his time in rehab. Definitely not worth it.

The food was healthy and mouth-watering; as a result, my body quickly healed. My noodle was still mixed up, though, and slower to come around. Living together in close proximity, doing six hours of courses a day, AA meetings, group therapy, individual counseling—talk about tense!

Two elements of the program really sucked. One was the three-meetings-a-day schedule of AA. The other was my attitude. I had a "play pocket pool" mind-set during the meetings. I didn't want to hear all these drunk-a-logs. It was all mental masturbation; I had no compassion for these incoherent pissing contests. Guys worse off than me bragging about their horror stories. It had nothing to do with my recovery; I was being forced to sit there and endure.

Fortunately, you can close your eyes but you can't close your ears. So, despite myself, sometimes and slowly I was rejoining the race we call human.

Sometimes I dared to feel progress. It was as though they were pouring me a hot bath but I would only put a toe in. At first I just couldn't open up. Part of me really wanted to, but the process required honesty. At the time I was incapable of being honest. I couldn't even find the fortitude to laugh at myself. I didn't have the strength to handle the blow.

Every meeting started with a prayer that brought back a memory of high school. The first funeral that I ever attended was for my best friend's dad. I never forgot it: the open casket, the first dead body I ever saw. At the funeral service, everyone said the Serenity Prayer, which is used to begin every AA meeting. That puzzled me. I'd never heard the prayer before—it wasn't in the funeral program—and yet most of the people at the service seemed to know it by heart. I even asked the widow, "Mother Tyler," about the prayer afterwards. She said that her husband, Bill, had been a recovering alcoholic. Sober for twenty years. That information was news to me. I thought of that moment every time the Fraser House AA meetings kicked off with "God, grant me..." In my mind I overlapped the concern about alcoholism with the image of a dead body laid out in a casket. In light of future events, that proved to be a rather freaky juxtaposition.

In time, the course picked up its own energy, and I got swept along. Bob started opening up. We are all progressing at our own speed. The staff was super; they didn't place any unrealistic demands on us. They put their whole emphasis on attraction rather than promotion. It was spooky—I began feeling concern for Jimmy and Stan, friendship for Douglas. I started shaving and brushing my teeth every day. I recognized when I was lying, when I was manipulating, and I saw what I was risking in being dishonest. I started taking the risk of letting people see the real me, taking off some of the Lon Chaney masks. Still full of guilt, still tentative, but there I was, experiencing honest feelings. Hard to believe. Insomnia is an old friend of mine, yet I was learning to sleep again.

Douglas and I walked for an hour every night. There were also baseball games, volleyball, all sorts of good stuff. My natural leadership qualities were resurfacing. I felt occasional bursts of confidence, which reminded me how much I'd lost. The weekends were tough, though. Douglas headed home after the first three weeks to visit with his family. Stan and Jimmy also visited their wives and family. But boB had no family. To him they were all dead, lost in the same disasters that had taken the best parts of his soul.

The rehabilitation process itself was all pretty new to me. The fact that alcoholism had recently been classified as a disease, and not as a character defect, was revolutionary. The counselors were testing new concepts on us. Most of all, they kept throwing the responsibility for redemption right back in our own laps. This approach worked for me. I found myself turning from class clown to teacher's pet. But as the weeks went by, I began to have some fears for my new buddies Moe, Larry, and Curly. They didn't seem to have the commitment to change that I had.

Sometimes the counselors would ask me about them, trying to get at the truth. Ometra was my answer. I'm no rat.

The last week of the course was freaky. I scored a job. Hot tar roofing. I had some experience with this kind of work—casual labor stints back in my early skid-row days. So a roofing company in Mission hired me to start work on the Monday after the course finished. That meant that I'd be staying on at Fraser House. After I got a couple of checks under my belt I could get off social assistance and find a room of my own.

The counselors wanted Douglas to spend a couple of extra weeks, too—there was so much to save. The family the house, the car were still there. He agreed. But Stan and Jimmy were champing at the bit to get the hell out of there. Not me. I considered Fraser House to be more good luck than I deserved, so I said thanks. I knew that my recovery was still underway. I was still consumed by guilt and self-blame. I hadn't yet realized that the past is a shared responsibility. As a result, I still loathed myself.

The road to recovery is dotted by the gravestones of those who don't make it. It's a sad fact that many are lost as they trudge along the happy road of destiny.

Even though the course was over, Douglas still couldn't roll his own cigarettes. Every night on our hour-long walk, I had to help him out. Through such simple dependencies we grew closer. Then, one night after work, he threw me a curve ball.

"Marg wants to have you come home for the weekend and stay with us."

"No way!"

"Bob, you're a good friend, you've helped me in my recovery, and I want to share you with my family. Don't be an asshole, Bob. They'll love you just like I do."

"Why would you want a bum like me in your home?"

"Isn't it about time you got on with your life, Bob? You're okay with me, and it's sad for me to see you still punishing yourself."

Yikes, I was floored. "Thanks a lot, but I have to work this weekend."

"Bullshit, Bob. You're coming."

I said, "I'll have to clear it with Fraser House."

"Great!" I found out later that the s.o.b. already had cleared it. I was doomed.

In a panic, I talked it over with my counselor. He said, "Go for it, you silly ass." So I did.

Hot Stuff

Hot-tar roofing is a dangerous job. Even after all these years, the smell of tar makes me want to puke.

As I said, I had experience with this kind of work, back in the old casual labor screw-up period. For a short while, I was paid every day to arrive one hour before a hot-tar crew and fire up the kettle. The kettle was a propane-fueled stove that melted fifty-pound kegs of solid tar. Water boils at two hundred twelve degrees Fahrenheit. But tar, with its stubborn specific gravity, has to reach three hundred degrees. One splash from the kettle was an instant skin barbecue.

On one particular day I arrived as usual—a pint in me and one on me—and fired up the kettle. Then I had to use the bathroom. So I crossed the street and went into one of those big-chain muffler shops. The young man said sure to the request for a key, and then he offered me a promotional cigar and the morning paper. I thanked him and proceeded to the throne room.

I sat there, puffing away like King Shit of Turd Island. *Perhaps,* I thought, *just a taste of the second pint. The day is going so well. A small sized libation. Just a lick!*

Sure, boB.

Sometime later, the muffler-shop employees started banging on the door. I finished the pint with alacrity. When I opened the door and looked across the street, I saw black smoke streaming from the kettle. Red flames were leaping into the sky like basketball players. I thought to myself: Wow, they *were* right. Hot tar DOES flash at three hundred twenty-five degrees.

Sirens heralded the arrival of the fire department and signaled my exit. I never did go back to pick up the two hundred dollars they owed me. Didn't seem right. Those vestiges haunting me again. Conscience, too.

Needless to say, I didn't tell my employer, Brett, in Mission about this tar-flashing episode.

Brett, the owner of the roofing company was a great worker but an insecure leader. He had real problems with his own authority and his relations with his employees. In other words, he was a jerk. One consequence of his personality was a big turnover of employees. That's why he worked so closely with Fraser House. The treatment center offered an inexhaustible supply of cannon-fodder crewmembers.

We worked cheap, too. As far as the pay schedule went, Brett followed the old custom of free enterprise— if you want monkeys for employees, pay peanuts. By the same token, beggars can't be choosers.

Pete was the name of the foreman, Brett's only full-time employee. Pete was a nice guy and a God-fearing man—a devout Mennonite who refused to be assertive. I tried to watch my language in front of Pete, out of respect for his convictions, but Brett's explosive behavior tested those convictions every day. Pete suffered with a Job-like patience.

Brett was no problem for me, by the way, because I was very assertive and had no convictions of any kind. Besides that, I was a super worker, fun to crew with, and prepared to take the pain to keep the job.

In fact, I was much better prepared for the pain of hot-tar roofing than for the terror of visiting a normal family home. Despite my nervousness, though, Douglas's family and I connected big-time. Instant bonding between the three children and me; likewise with Marg, his wife. Robby, their natural child, was twelve. Angela, adopted, was older by eight months. In other words, Robby was something of a miracle. Douglas and Marg had been told that they would never conceive a child, so they adopted Angela. Then, eight months later, Robby was born. Later they also adopted a native Indian girl named Annie, who was about to turn nine. I had showed up in time for Annie's birthday party. Great stuff!

Angela had a pre-pubescent crush on me, and she became a good buddy. She knew I was doing good stuff for her dad.

Robby was into football with a passion. As I said, I had been on several championship lacrosse teams and gone to the BC Lions' training camp. So Robby latched onto me as his personal trainer. I taught him cut-back blocking, pass blocking. All sorts of good football skills. He worshipped the ground I walked on.

A few months later, Douglas and Marg trusted me with their children when they went to Seattle for a weekend. Trusted ME! With their children! Me! I became the "Dutch uncle," closer even than that. Over the ensuing months, I took the children everywhere—swimming pools, the movies (*Bad News Bears*), roller skating, Birch Bay. I taught them how to crab. We hiked, camped on the shore of a wilderness beach, had a huge fire, ate junk food and drank sodas. Life was coming together for me. I bought a Suzuki motorcycle. I was cool again—just like the Fonz on *Happy Days*.

Douglas, however, was not being cool. He could not surrender the relationship with Ethyl; he regressed. Beer only, then hard liquor only, then he switched to wine only... The false dawn of chronic alcoholism lit the sky. I felt responsible. He was my only friend. I prayed for him, asked God to take me instead, but nothing worked. Soon his lumberyard job vanished, and so did two more jobs over the next nine months. This was a difficult time for me, too, but I hung on by going to meetings. I stayed sober by a thread.

Meanwhile, the roofing job was going great. By now I was Brett's second steady employee. In less than five months I was running my own crew. I'm a lucky guy! Things come easy to me. I learned quickly how to work a crew and maximize its productivity. The secret. Lead by example. And remember that warm fuzzies always work better than degrading, negative bullshit. The proof was in my crew's productivity. We kicked ass because we were a team—a concept far removed from Brett's hot-head style of constant ragging on his employees. I told Brett to stay the fuck away from my people or I was history.

Brett was making tons of dough, so he cut me some slack. Having a workaholic foreman didn't hurt the growth-curve. Hell, I created his growth-curve—Pete told me that piece of information. Things come easy to me; I am leader. This is not to brag but to enlighten. It's fun to be in my jet stream, taking my lead.

Pete was growing up a bit, too. He actually talked back to Brett occasionally. Cute is the best way to describe it. After a confrontation with the boss, Pete would actually strut, for hours. He'd give me a wink, and I would acknowledge by smiling and giving a thumbs-up sign.

Then my crew had an unfortunate accident—rather, one member of the team did. He was a young man from Quebec, recently hired by Brett as a shingle roofer. This was Brett's new ambition—to expand his horizons beyond hot-tar roofing to include asphalt and shingle work. At first, though, Brett didn't have enough work in the new guy's specialty. So when he wasn't swinging a hammer, Shingles would crew along with us.

This asshole quickly proved to be brain-dead.

Because he was a rookie to hot-tar work, I had him start, as was traditional, on the kettle. But he kept taking his shirt off. Facing the kettle with a bare chest is not only stupid, it's also against the Workers Compensation Board work rules. I threatened, I explained, I tried everything in my bag of tricks. I even told him to go home—he wouldn't go! I told Brett about the problem; so did Pete. But Brett chose not to do anything. So screw it, I finally decided.

This is the way I saw it. The guy is a jerk-off. I have a roofing team. If I have to baby-sit one guy who won't do as he's told, I compromise the integrity of the team. Then the whole thing falls apart. So, although I continued to chirp at him every day about this dangerous practice, in reality I gave up expecting any good to come of it. You just can't get through to some people.

When the kettle blew, though, and hot tar claimed his face and his torso, I felt sick inside. When he started screaming, I started wishing I'd done something—used a shotgun, the police, anything—to keep that bastard off the construction site. We finally got him tackled down, and we could see right away that he'd be needing new skin and a new self-image. Disfigurement is sickening. The smell of burned flesh is also a gagger. Make that boiled flesh, it gags too.

When Brett found out, he went berserk. Brainless ballistic Brett—it was his nature to blame. The crew all defended me, but Brett wasn't listening. So I calmly told Brett that I was booking off. He could call me at Fraser House that night if he wanted me back at the job. I left. That night I went to the hospital to see Shingles. It wasn't pretty. The man was out-to-lunch on pain killers, including morphine. The doctor told me that they would be doing skin transplants, then plastic surgery. I felt anger but also pity—no one deserves to be disfigured, even if they are stupid.

Naturally, Brett was too proud to phone.

But the next morning Brett called and started hitting on me for not being at work.

I told him, "It's been a slice. Thanks for taking a chance on a recovering alcoholic. Please make up my check."

He backtracked, but I was adamant. No, I wouldn't reconsider. He even got Pete to call me. It made me realize that alcoholics aren't the only ones who know how to use and manipulate.

Monkeys and peanuts.

And so the ranks of the unemployed grew by one. Big deal! At least I could see evidence that my self-respect was returning. And I learned again, as I have learned over and over, that sobriety doesn't guarantee smooth sailing.

I moved out to Richmond to be closer to Douglas, in case he wanted someone to talk to. His downward spiral was accelerating. He needed me. When you have me for a friend, you're stuck with me. I even visit you in hospital. This is not a bad thing having me for a friend.

The most poignant memory I have of this time is being in a bar with Douglas. He was buying drinks for everyone; I was drinking soda. "My son Robby plays football. He's made all-star," he bragged. "My friend Bob taught Robby everything. The big game is today: can't wait to see how good he'll be."

"Douglas, come on. We've got to get going. The game starts soon." I was almost begging. Finally, I excused myself. "Well, I'm leaving. I don't want to miss the kick-off."

"Yeah, yeah, I'll catch up with you at the game," Douglas said.

As I left the bar, I saw him pick up his glass, turn to his drinking buddy, and continue to brag about Robby. Frustrated, I fired up my bike, did a wheelie, and left in a cloud of burned rubber. The kick-off was all set to go. Just as I arrived, the kids broke the huddle and took the field.

Douglas never made it to the game.

Robby's team won on the strength of his two touchdowns. He and I had worked out a counter play that sent him alone to the left when the team did a right sweep. We called it "The Hidden Route." On his first touchdown, there was nobody within ten yards of him. On the second, he carried two guys into the end zone.

Every time Robby did something heroic, he'd look over at the stands to see if his dad had finally arrived. Marg was upset and worried; she couldn't understand what could have happened to Douglas. I knew. Too much alcohol had happened to Douglas.

When we got back to the house, there he was—fast asleep in his bed. The victory celebration invaded the house minutes later. Robby put on a good front, but I knew he was devastated.

Even my friendship hadn't helped. Douglas was in big trouble, heavy danger. The cure for alcoholism, I had learned, comes from within. The choice was Douglas's to make; I was powerless to make it for him. First he had to accept his condition, and then he had to choose not to drink. Honest acceptance and then a decision to do something about it.

Douglas still, even now, did not think he was powerless over alcohol. I knew, though, and was distraught.

One Step Back

I was living with three young men, friends of Douglas. They had worked with him at the lumberyard. We were sharing accommodations in a condo in Richmond, a bedroom community just minutes outside Vancouver. I was smoking joints now and then to take the edge off. The weight of Douglas's drinking condition was a big heavy mess. I called almost every day. But I didn't go over every day; it was too painful. My relationship with the children didn't suffer. We still went places together and had fun times.

I now owned a nineteen seventy-two Meteor—an old pig, but it ran well enough. Still had "my baby," the motorcycle. I found great peace driving it. I'd get up on the dike in Richmond and open it up, racing along with a huge ditch on one side of me and the open sea on the other. Here, the ocean breezes were sweet and clean, unlike the marshy thickness of Vancouver, heavy with the sense of decomposition. Or I'd take my bike up into the forest and run free, come out at the top of a hill, and feast my senses on the green of Fraser River Valley, the smell of cedar trees, the rustling sounds of alder leaves in the wind.

Jobs were easy to find. I still used casual labor. But now the employers called and asked specifically for me. They paid me to select my own team from the casual labor pool and transport the men myself to the site. They paid me to supervise the crew as we worked together.

I started going to singles dances. I even got laid. Sex is a lot better when you're sober. At least, it must be a lot better for my partner when I'm sober, because every gal invited me back for seconds, thirds...

Here's the truth. A large percentage of the women come to these dances specifically for the promise of good sex. Their ex-husbands are alcoholics. They all have the experience of coupling with their lawfully-wedded booze-hounds. As my dear old mother used to say, liquor enhances the desire but takes away the performance. One feisty gal kept harping on the theme. "Like trying to get a marsh-mellow into a piggy bank," she kept saying. These ladies were easy pickin's.

Why in the world would I want to drink?

In fact, Bob had a great edge over boB, and he was using it to full advantage. Besides that, life was good enough. Livable, at least!

Then on one ordinary Saturday, rather early in the morning, Marg called. Douglas had gone into the hospital last night. Stomach pains. And then at three in the morning he died.

It was a thunderbolt to the heart and mind. I remember little else of the conversation. She told me the cause of his death, but after she hung up I couldn't remember. I told her I'd be over in fifteen minutes.

It took me half an hour. I couldn't stop crying, and my body felt numb. I rode the Suzuki. The children were there, and Marg's parents and her brother. I felt as frail as a hollow egg.

I hugged the children. We all had red swollen eyes. I had trouble concentrating on what people were saying. Actually, I must have been in shock—numb, angry, and sad all at the same time. I felt grief, the whole gamut of emotions.

My behavior was weird enough that Marg said—"Bob, have you been drinking?"

The question shocked me, but I brushed it off. She was in grief, I figured, and saying crazy things. I just said, "No." But my response should have been "Not yet!"

Douglas died because one of his internal organs gave up. The liver or the pancreas. I can't remember. The doctor blamed alcohol, which caused fluid retention and overtaxed the organ. In fact, the doctor had warned Douglas that the booze had to stop.

Still, he'd chosen to drink. That was a selfish choice made by a sick man.

Douglas was an alcoholic. He never accepted that fact completely. Because he didn't, booze killed him. It orphaned his kids. It left his family and his friends shattered.

I had to get out of there fast. I drove aimlessly. Went down to the ocean, threw rocks in the sea, got angry, angry at God! Why him, and not me? Then I made a loser decision, went to the liquor store, got a bottle, and went back to the beach. I threw away the cap and drank the bottle, smashed the empty, and returned to Skid Road.

Another room with a plastic mattress cover and no window. My domain. Where I deserved to be. I made a run to the liquor store on foot. I told myself I was just going to hole up for a few days with the car parked. Compose myself. Do some planning. Get back on track. Work things out.

Bullshit. I chose to drink because the reality of Douglas's death was more than I was willing to endure. Numb doesn't hurt. When things got tough, I copped out and hid in a bottle.

Hid in a bottle? Oh sure, boB. Now you're really shoveling the bullshit. You're wallowing in it now. Poor you! Douglas chose to drink. You are not responsible.

The only really memorable thing about this drunk was a statement that a couple of guys made at one of the old watering holes. "Bob, we haven't seen you around for a few weeks." The truth was, I hadn't been around for eighteen months.

My, how the time flies when you're having fun!

I missed the funeral because I was too drunk. It was a selfish choice. I thought about that for a couple of days. And then I decided that it was either suicide or detox. One or the other.

I did the Ben Franklin close to help me decide.

The Ben Franklin close? It's a salesman's term. Let me explain.

When Franklin, that famous American, needed to make important decisions, he used this technique—draw a line down the center of a blank piece of paper and write "Reasons To" on the left and "Reasons Not To" on the right. Pro and con. Stack them up. The side with the most reasons wins.

You can decide with a ruler.

It's a simple but powerful tool for closing a sale, and it's just as powerful when you're deciding whether or not to self-destruct— especially when you're demented with grief and cast down into terrible hopelessness over your incurable alcoholism. An objective method makes the decision-making process easy. Sorry, Ben, here we go.

Reasons To Kill Myself:
    Insanity rules.
    The whole joke of life is over.
    I'll have no more worries about trying to live sober.
    I'll be out of my misery.
    My conscious mind won't be ravaged by the pain of failure.
    No rent.
    No more work.
    No more pain.
    Douglas's death.
    No more risks.
    No more seizures,
    No more hospitals,
    No more detox.
    No more guilt. No more classrooms, no more crooks, no more teachers' dirty looks. School's out!

Glug, glug.
    I was supposed to go on then to the "Reasons Not To," but my mind shifted. I couldn't come up with any. Alas, all pros, no cons.
    Glug, glug, glug. Oblivion!

I came back to consciousness still very depressed. By this point in the adventure, I wasn't even getting out of bed. I was just waking up angry, then drinking, then passing out again. But this time I remembered the Ben Franklin close. And then I had a moment of clarity. (Nothing about alcoholism makes any sense.) I decided to settle the matter with the flip of a coin. Detox or death—so what?
    Heads, detox. Tails death.
    Detox won.
    I tried to get up but I couldn't.
    Glug, glug. I passed out again. Finally the booze was pretty well gone. I walked the mile to detox. God knows how I made it. I stopped in several bars for cool beers. They admitted me into detox. I seizured, hallucinated, did a lot of puking.
    You do the crime, you do the time, asshole. It's that *déjà vu* happening all over again. Ha fucking ha!
    Sitting there in detox, I suffered through a huge guilt withdrawal. Then more guilt. Anger. Unrealistic fears. I called Marg

and the children to apologize. To let them know I was okay. They were relieved; they'd been afraid for me. Robby said, "Dad wouldn't want you to drink, Bob. He was so proud of your sobriety." You can imagine how this made me feel.

So I went to one of the staff members and asked for help again. I was beginning to learn just how powerless I am over alcohol. Detox fixed it for me to go to Maple Ridge, another treatment center. Even after I sobered up, I remembered the Franklin close and the toss of the coin. My options were limited to two. Without help I would have killed myself, rather than go back on the treadmill of Skid Road. Treatment had to be my salvation, or else.

And nothing very memorable happened at Maple Ridge, I listened a lot better. Some more knowledge about alcoholism sunk in. The realization that I would never be able to drink normally was slowly pushing its way into my brain. I passed the course. I was still healing from Douglas's death. I still am.

I applied for a job in the oil sands at Fort McMurray, in the far northern wilds of Alberta. I contacted Bill, the engineer who once helped Garry dig me out of the sawdust in the bin accident back at the lumber mill. He knew about my breakdown and my alcohol abuse, and he was happy to help me—now that I was sober— with a letter of recommendation. By now he was the chief engineer at Woodfiber, a large pulp and paper mill. His letter secured the position for me. I'd be working as an insulator, lagging pipes to keep the heat in. It was similar to the bin man's job back at the power house.

Right about this time, I heard about Jimmy. The news came about a week before I left for the oil sands job.

The hard-core Irishman had gone right back into the sauce the same day he left Fraser House. So had Stan. Treatment only works when you want it bad enough, I guess. Eventually Jimmy drank his way out of a job, and while he was down he had a stroke. The stroke left him crippled down the left side of his body. He became a permanent ward of the government.

I visited him once before I left for Alberta. Gone was the Irish lilt, gone the beautiful tenor singing voice. Removed by the Witchy Bitch. I don't suppose he lived long after, though. He had too much pride.

I knew I'd never go visit him again. I was angry and frustrated. Just memories of Jimmy left now. I loved the guy, temper and all.

I didn't know where Stan was—only knew that he was back at 'er, and that his wife had left him. The hell of it was that I felt guilty, being the only one who'd made a year-plus sober. Good grief. No prisoners taken in Ethyl's liquidarium. Sometimes she screws up and only maims; more often, Ethyl kills. That old gang of mine is pretty well gone—never forgotten—just dead or permanently maimed.

Staying Cool

"Get hooked up with some AA meetings," said Tim, my counselor from Maple Ridge, when he dropped me off at Vancouver International Airport. "Remember, your sobriety comes first. Everything you want will happen—if you choose to stay sober and let it."

We hugged, and I boarded the Pacific Western flight that would transport me to the Oil Sands of Alberta. The first plane ride was going to take me east a thousand miles over the Rockies to the great central plains. The second plane, from Edmonton, would then take me north into Santa Claus country. Sure, I was anxious. More than being anxious, though, I was really fed up with failure and with booze. This could be my new start.

The climate I was leaving is classified as "West Coast Marine"—in other words, wet, mild, and moldy—and the date was the fifth of January. In the natural order of things, skies were supposed to be gray and soggy. So my first glimpse of Edmonton through the plane window was a surprise.

Greater Edmonton is a city of four hundred thousand plus, and it lies three hundred fifty miles north of Montana. To locate you globally, Edmonton is on the same latitude as Murmansk in Russia.

The world shone brilliantly. The snow's whiteness magnified the already intense sunlight a hundred-fold. The sky was such a vivid blue that I just kept staring at it like a fool. In that penetrating sky, plumes of steam billowed upwards hundreds of feet. No, thousands—the exhaust of the heating systems in high-rise buildings.

After we landed, I went to the hiring agent, Bechtel, and picked up my ticket for the next plane to the job site at Fort McMurray. After the necessary paperwork, I had time to kill, so I decided to kick back and explore the city of Edmonton on foot. But when I stepped outside, the wind hit me like a school bus. I was absolutely unprepared for the paralyzing effects of minus-thirty-five degrees Fahrenheit.

The snow danced across the streets in waves shaped by the wind—like a cross between *Lawrence of Arabia* and *Nanook of the North*. I was afraid to breathe. I spit, and it froze in mid-air. My body had never experienced the clear possibility that it was about to freeze to death, that the wind would frostbite fingers to the bone if I dared to pull them out of my mittens.

All the parked cars were still running. I asked and found out why. When you shut them off, they're parked until May.

The air was as dry as any desert. When cars accelerated from stoplights, they spewed clouds of condensation. These clouds of fog engulfed the cars behind, blinding drivers for several seconds. I could feel the snot freezing in my nose. I kept wondering how the aboriginal Indians survived here.

Wow. True cold. Blue balls cold. Cold that you could hear. Power lines buzzed as though they were shivering. Cars creaked and groaned in ways I'd never heard before. Everybody's brakes had a brittle squeal.

The bloody river was frozen—four feet of solid ice! When I ducked into stores to warm up, condensation on my glasses froze solid. I had to breathe on them until the lenses thawed. This took several minutes. Then, after I warmed up, I was back at it, walking around, testing my limits in the cold. The plane wasn't leaving until after dark.

Raw unfiltered sunlight reflected off the snow and then magnified in the air. Welcome to the Great White North, Bottlehopper.

The plane to Fort McMurray was filled with lads from Newfoundland. They kept shouting, "Lord flamin' Jesus baley."

Newfies are a hard-drinking bunch, and their passion is called "screech"—homemade booze from a rum base. Moonshine with a kick like a mule. I'd never sampled the stuff, but it looked as though these boys certainly had before boarding. Like all good old boys from the backwoods, the Newfies loved to party and had no fear. Nothing complicated with these boys. A spade is a shovel. Problems were settled with fisticuffs. I kept thinking of Jimmy.

They accepted me even though I didn't drink.

It was a short flight; only three hundred fifty miles. But it was three hundred fifty miles due north. Imagine going to the Canadian border of Montana. Then keep going another six hundred and fifty miles.

Here the great plains once formed an inland sea—hence, they contained vast deposits of oil and gas. Incredibly, at the oil sands of Fort McMurray; the black gold bubbles to the surface just the way it did for Jed Clampett.

A bus picked us up at the airport and took us to the Syncrude site, adjacent to Mildred Lake. The job site was actually a small city inhabited by ten thousand workmen. Ten thousand! I kept wondering how they kept track of everyone. How they fed them all. The logistics of the operation boggled me, especially in this cruel white cold.

This was already a great adventure. And not only were they giving me the chance to live and work here, but they were also offering good money. The pay for insulators was nearly fourteen dollars an hour, plus shift differential. The food and lodging were included. We worked ten-hour days, six days a week. The company paid overtime for anything over a forty-hour week. You can do the calculations; when it comes to mathematics, I'm like the author—a Dumass. I only know that this was big bucks back in 1978, when the minimum wage was three and a half dollars an hour.

The company bus delivered us to our individual billets, one per room, and I hit the sack. Slept like a log; probably worn out from all that walking I'd done in Edmonton. The next day was orientation. The camp manager, or "campy," woke us and directed us to breakfast. Here, you ate at your appointed minute or not at all.

The campy was an old rounder. He needed a shave, and he smelled of cigarette butts and stale booze. He told us right away who to see for bootleg. Imagine that, a bootlegger—and we hadn't even had breakfast yet! The old boB would have thought he'd died and gone to heaven.

Orientation took most of the morning. We watched a documentary about oil. Top-end oil is amber in color; it has a high percentage of gasoline in it. The benchmark is Texas crude. But here at Fort McMurray, we were dealing with bottom-end stuff sticky-black guck. This stuff was very valuable for making plastics. The place contained zillions of barrels of oil. Unfortunately, the oil was locked in miles-deep sand. Our challenge was to extract the oil from the sand in this hostile environment.

The scale of everything at Fort McMurray was monstrous. The drag line, for example—a machine for scooping up the oil-rich sand—gobbled up a hundred cubic tons with every bite. Basically, it was an enormous arm and bucket, something like on a backhoe, which a gargantuan system of pulleys and cables dragged out to the sand pits and back again. Every other machine seemed somehow proportionate to the drag line. Truck tires were eight feet or more in diameter. An elaborate system of conveyor belts brought the sand to the retorts. The retorts, huge pressure-cookers, accepted the sand and blasted the oil free in their steam. Then long conveyor belts returned the clean sand to the pit, and the drag line gouged out another maw-full. Black oil kept oozing up from below. According to the best guess, the oil sands could sustain themselves like this for another five or six hundred years. The documentary film convinced me that extraction process was kind to the environment, energy efficient, and—on a scale of large—almost impossible to comprehend, let alone put into words.

Then we got lectures about booze, drugs, and gambling. The speakers came from the Alberta Alcohol and Drug Abuse Commission—AADAC, for short. Using booze or drugs on the job site was cause for immediate dismissal. If we had substance-abuse problems, we were encouraged to attend the active AA and NA programs on site. We were also encouraged to report on any workers who were getting high on the job.

They warned us about gambling, too. Big money was being earned, so big-money card games threatened the camp's stability. Twenty thousand dollars on the turn of a card. Major-league competition. We heard about some workers had suffered heavy losses and killed themselves.

"Why are you giving us all this information?" someone asked.

"Because of the large turn over of employees," said the counselor. "It costs the company lots of money to get you guys here, and the company wants you to stay."

That was our orientation. In short, the environment was spooky for a recovering alcoholic. There was even a pub on site, with bus service every half hour. Over three hundred seats. God, grant me the serenity...

I learned to do the McMurray shuffle. I'll explain. The secret to working in extreme cold is this: don't sweat. If you get sweaty, you get chills, and the chills make you miserable. So you learn to layer your clothing. That way you can strip off layers whenever you feel your body-heat rising, and you avoid big outbursts of exertion. Above all, you don't want to walk so fast that your body gets steamed up inside your protective clothing. So when you walk, you do a slow shuffle. We also called it the McMurray two-step.

I lasted two months before I had a beer. I didn't get drunk, but I realized that I had to get out of that environment. I talked with the foreman. They flew me back to Edmonton with money in my pocket and I had no idea what to do next.

It seemed to me that Bob did better in a controlled environment. The treatment center, for example. The Oil Sands was just too tempting for me at this stage of my recovery. It took me many years to gain the strength in sobriety to say no. And I needed longer than that to begin feeling comfortable as a sober alcoholic. For me, sobriety was an unnatural state. If you're an alcoholic, it feels normal to be drinking.

While I was back in Edmonton trying to figure out what to do next, I started hearing about the High Arctic—about drilling for oil on Arctic islands and also on offshore ice platforms. I began asking around. Are the camps dry? No booze allowed, I was told. That was good enough for me.

I figured I could hire on in any capacity and then rise to the top like cream. The work ethic. Go for it. The kid from the Royal City was trudging the happy road of destiny, and the road was leading way up north of Alaska. Above the Arctic Circle, into total isolation and safety.

I could function when there was no booze. No booze. No problem saying no.

Harry Truman said, "If you can't stand the heat, get out of the kitchen," and that's what I did. I have to say that I was surprised at my own ability to put the demon back in the bottle and leave Fort McMurray. The Bottlehopper was moving forward, gaining confidence, and learning to run like hell when he felt vulnerable.

I scored a job with a large catering firm. They put me out in a camp just north of Edmonton to give me a test-run. I proved myself in only six weeks. Like so many things in life, all it took was hard work. Then, back in Edmonton, they ran me through a thorough medical exam, including a stool sample. "What the hell is this for?" I asked.

"Looking for parasitic worms."

No worms! So I got the job. Camp attendant.

I was booked off to Rae Point, the base camp for all High-Arctic exploration, and from there to one of the three rigs farther north. Out there, we were as isolated as people can be. Even the Inuit and the Aleut lived hundreds of miles south. The nearest liquor store was four hundred miles away. The basic law of supply and demand was strictly enforced here; there was no supply, so you couldn't demand. Smoke was readily available—pot, hash, and hash oil that you could paint on a cigarette. I snorted coke once—through a hundred dollar bill, no less. Made my nose feel frozen. I preferred pot or hash. I never did take any up with me, but I was offered lots, and sometimes I used it.

At Banks Island, where I was sent, the temperature ranged anywhere between minus thirty degrees and something close to death itself. Reality was turned on its head. The sun failed to show up for six months at a time. When it finally appeared, it bobbed over the horizon at about twenty degrees—and there it stayed twenty-four hours a day. Stars were in the wrong place. The silence was palpable. The environment was pristine, mostly cold and clear.

Lots of guys got cabin fever. They had to be flown out. Just couldn't hack the isolation! The twenty-four-hour-a-day darkness really messed up the metabolism of some of the work-hands. Twenty-four-hour-a-day sunlight was just as maddening. We found that if we put black plastic garbage bags on all the windows, it was better than seeing daylight at three in the morning.

Although some men suffered, the contrary Bottlehopper thrived. The environment was hostile, but the food was exquisite. And we had to eat a lot of it. The simple act of breathing burned a lot of fuel, so the camp recommended an average daily caloric intake of six thousand calories. We worked twelve hours on and twelve hours off. That gave me a decent amount of time to explore and ask questions, and to play hearts, bridge, and rummy. In my former life, I was a voracious reader; now I could catch up on years of current events. (I remember discovering that Lyndon Johnson had died several years before.) Most of all, I could be productive and enjoy my work with no fear.

I'm a lucky guy, eh?

The camp at Banks Island was a booze-free zone for nearly everyone. But one special population had a penchant for making their own moonshine. These were the native Inuit and Aleut who were hired to work in the camp as game monitors, "go-fers," and other menial roles. Being resourceful, they concocted their own brew using Lysol, Tang crystals, raisins, yeast, and God knows what else. They'd let the mix ferment for a week or so, then swill it down. I never sampled the stuff, but it worked. Those imbibing were always under the weather.

I enjoyed working with these young native men. They were a fun bunch, as playful and unrestrained as big children. I don't mean to be demeaning in saying that. I just didn't know how else to explain some of the mischievous things they'd do.

For example, it wasn't clear to me why they decided to piss in the camp's snow melter. The snow melter was a gas-fired steel box that we filled continuously with snow to be melted down to water. This was water for personal use; the whole camp needed it, including the two young natives whose job it was to fill the melter. I don't know what misunderstanding led them to empty their bladders into the tank, too, but the Tool Push was furious when he caught them at it. Imagine the hassle. The cistern inside the camp had to be drained and all the water lines flushed, especially those to the kitchen.

Someone else started taking people's jewelry. Suddenly watches, rings, and gold necklaces were disappearing from the washroom. The work hands would shave first and leave their jewelry out on the counter while they showered; it would be gone when they came out. It never vanished from their kits; only if it was left out. After much to-do, the culprit was found. He was a young aboriginal who said, "The stuff was just lying there like no one wanted it, so I just took it!" I was half inclined to believe him. They ran him off, fired him.

Child-like. Tell you what—those little guys could sure kick, though. Twice their height at least from a standing kick.

Alcohol abuse is a huge problem among the indigenous people of the North. In fact, Ethyl A's wicked spells seem to have an especially destructive power over indigenous populations no matter where you go. This is the plight of native Indians in North America, Mexico, and South America and the scourge of the aboriginals of Australia and all the Pacific Islands, including Hawaii. Muslims always show a low percentage of alcoholics in any study. But alcohol is forbidden by the Koran—which is a good thing, because Muslims who drink exhibit one of the world's highest rates of addiction. East Indians are in the same category. "High risk" is too mild a classification for these people. The statistics are terrifying. This could be a doctoral thesis—alcohol abuse is an international problem of enormous significance. It is a plague upon our species.

By the way, Banks Island is home to lots of non-human species, too. I was amazed to find out how many. Mammals actually thrive in this hostile environment. Warm water currents make this one of the best places in the Arctic for observing wildlife.

Carnivorous rabbits called Arctic hares are nothing like Bambi's Thumper, believe me. These bloody bunnies are about three feet tall. The Arctic Fox was by far the most handsome animal. He looked like a white powder puff. Wolves, plenty of them, roamed around us in packs.

Lemmings were abundant, filling out the bottom end of the food chain.

I never saw one bird this far north.

Once I saw a polar bear up close—dead. He'd been hanging around the camp. The camp's Inuit game managers had tried to chase it away. Finally they had to shoot it. Polar bears are protected by law—their fur is extremely valuable on the black market—so fish-and-wildlife personnel flew out to supervise the killing and to remove the carcass. This was a young one, only eight feet from nose to foot.

Fortunately, I never got up close and personal with a live one. Polar bears are the largest carnivores in North America, and they're smart. They learned how to stalk the long walk between the camp and the oil rig. We had to live at least a mile from the rig to be safe if it hit sour gas or had a blow-out or flare. It was a dangerous walk and we all knew it. The bears would nest in the area until the right conditions prevailed. Wildlife officers could tell how long a bear had "nested up" by the amount of stool it had deposited. Then we'd have a white-out—the polar equivalent of a sand storm. No visibility. That's when the bear would strike, leaving behind nothing but a hard-hat and a patch of frozen blood.

During the spring break-up in the McKenzie delta, the polar bears would come traveling down river riding the ice floes. If one of these floes struck one of our floating rigs, the bears would disembark and begin stalking. Rig workers would simply disappear.

I'll never forget the specimen that walked through camp one day. It passed me on the other side of a four-foot-high flatbed trailer. I could see all of its back as it cruised by; it must have been twelve feet long.

Now that I think about it, the sight of a polar bear now and then is probably a good thing for any recovering alcoholic. One of the biggest problems in recovery is boredom. On Banks Island, boredom was not an issue.

I used to take the quad, an all-terrain vehicle, and go harass the musk oxen. I was surprised to see how small they are. As I drove up, they would form a defensive circle with the females and the young in the center and the bulls face out, horns at the ready. Picture the Bottlehopper, driving around and around the musk oxen in the high Arctic desert, through granular snow eons old.

One day I walked on the ice in a place where no one had ever walked before and probably no one ever would again. Neil Armstrong, stand back. The Bottlehopper was touching a last frontier.

It was a good feeling.

When I looked ahead, though, I felt some trepidation. Whether I wanted it or not, I had to take two weeks off. That was the contract—six weeks in and two weeks out. They made you go out. Two weeks in Edmonton with a pocket full of money. Yikes!

God, I was scared stiff! The hotel scene had been the center of my universe for so many years. The thought of hanging around in bars and drinking soda. Just because I was lonely.

One fact was certain. "Bob, if you hang around with dogs, you're gonna get fleas." Simple as that!

Of Slips and Slides

As social animals, we need interaction with our own kind. It's the herd instinct. The problem with me now, however was finding my herd. By now the only socializing I could recall was in and around the hotel-bar scene. The bar scene had been my universe. If I was flush, I lived in a hotel, ate there, mingled there, slept there, and occasionally got lucky there.

My third trip into town with a pocketful of money resulted in my getting laid and slipping back to drinking. I went the whole way and got drunk. Drunk for most of five days. Except for the sex at the beginning, it was a lousy time.

I should have remembered about the macho dog. This canine was crossing the railway tracks as slow as you please in the face of an oncoming train. He had an attitude—he was just too big a dog to go out of his way for some crummy little train. But he sauntered just a little too slowly. His body made it across, but the steel wheels of the train cut off his tail. Startled, the dog turned around to see what had happened to his tail. In a heartbeat, the next set of wheels cut off his head. Like him, I should have re-membered not to lose my head over a piece of tail.

That's a cute story. But I'm lying again. I didn't lose my head over a piece of tail. I chose to drink.

At least I'm learning to be honest again.

While I was drunk, I was consumed by anger, guilt, and self-loathing. I might as well have walked around flagellating myself. I knew sobriety; I enjoyed sobriety—even so, I'd screwed up. That was a heavy load.

Finally the gray matter prevailed, and I don't know why but this idiot ended up seeking help, starting with a sobering-up in detox.

The first thing that happens in detox is that you are processed—last name first, first name last. The rubber room (the front office, receiving area) is a crummy place. The staff leave you in there to find out if you're prepared to tough it out once withdrawal commences. That usually takes five or more hours. And then you start to shake and sweat. Quite often, especially if you have some coin left, you walk. You know that a drink will settle you down—temporarily at least. The windows are reinforced with metal wire, and staff members monitor the room constantly.

The rubber room is a self-torture chamber, the official home of petit mal seizures, grand mal seizures, and the DTs. Epileptic fits are part of the show. You never recall your own, though—you just regain consciousness feeling disorganized. Sometimes you damage yourself: biting yourself in the mouth, tongue, and lips; you gash yourself falling on chairs or banging into the floor. You end up with stitches in your tongue and your scalp.

I remember one time back at the Sally Anne Hostel when I was eating my bowl of soup after singing for my supper. A guy at the next table hit the deck with a seizure. The thirty or so drunks in the room all stopped eating and watched the floor show. Then, suddenly, two more hit the deck. Now we had three flopping around. While the three men flopped, I started clapping my hands and humming a Ukrainian folk song. Next thing I knew, the rest of the place was doing the same thing, clapping and stomping their feet. In a room full of drunks, epilepsy is contagious, and so is a sick sense of humor.

In detox, some patients get Dilantin; others phenobarbital, I think. This weary traveler from the Royal City always got Dilantin. I suppose the central nervous system short-circuits. That's all I know about this phenomenon. The bloody things came without warning. If I felt hot or upset, my mood seemed to precipitate the attacks.

There were delusions, too. I saw some pretty neat things. You've already met my mute Irish friend. But he was just one character in a whole cartoon world. If I stared at a blank wall, I got TV. Sometimes I saw scary things like snakes and spiders; sometimes past-life scenes with people who didn't answer when I talked to them. Like my Irish pal, the hallucinations were always mute.

After the first few times, I learned to sit back and enjoy the show. The real problem wasn't believing the hallucinations, but doubting everything else. Once I saw a bottle of Black Velvet whiskey in the rubber room, under a chair across the room from me. The bloody thing looked so real! Get a life, Bottlehopper, I kept thinking—the rubber room doesn't sell booze. But after an hour the black cylinder was still there.

Finally I asked the supervisor, "Please come look. I think there's a bottle under that chair."

She laughed, but then she got off her butt and looked. Sure enough. She reached down, and her grasping hand turned my delusion into a reality. Somebody must have bolted from detox so bewildered that he forgot his own bottle of temporary relief. I imagined him getting halfway down the street and then suddenly remembering.

I was never sure of anything in the rubber room. Once I saw a fifty-dollar bill on the floor. I looked to see if anyone was watching, then I bent down to get it. Suddenly a little gargoyle character came out of the wall, grabbed it, and disappeared back into the wall.

That shook me up.

Sometimes I would purposely induce the hallucinations by staring intently at the wall; more often than not I was able to see color pictures of my family and friends. They never spoke. Just flashing pictures, sometimes still, sometimes moving. I was never freaked out by these visions. They were cool, quite unreal and therefore harmless.

What the heck. They helped me pass the time.

Passing time was the main occupation of everybody in the rubber room. Consequently, the place had a communal atmosphere characterized by bravado—Y-chromosome bullshit and, as they say, pissing contests. Guys claiming that they could drink three fifths of whiskey a day—a physical impossibility. Sometimes there was enough coherence in the room to get up a game of bridge. Sometimes there wasn't enough smarts in the room to play old maid.

I participated in the banter and games because time went better. My last time in detox, though, I stayed out. I looked around and thought, "I don't belong here. This part of my life is over." The feeling was real. And good. "These people are losers, unless they make a decision to change." I said to myself.

But I could see myself manifested in every one of them. So I stayed for the cure.

If you were still in the rubber room after six hours of this, the staff took you for a shower. They took your clothes away and washed them, and then they assigned you to a bed. The next day you were monitored closely by the nursing staff. Blood pressure, pulse. Standard stuff.

Sometimes they'd have to send you to the hospital. That happened to me a couple of times—pneumonia, blood poisoning, and dehydration.

If not, on the second day you were moved to a permanent room and integrated into the schedule of recovery. A nurse was on staff, and a medical doctor visited twice a week. Starting with day one, and then every day, you attended AA meetings. You listened, although the message rarely sank in. After a couple more days, you were eating and starting to come around. Usually after seven days you were cut loose.

I had my own way of knowing when I was almost well. One of the nurses had great buns. As soon as I started having delusions of grandeur over those buns, I realized it was time to leave.

That's detox, folks.

This time after detox I went right back to the controlled environment of the Arctic. I was quite happy to return to the safety of a new camp called Whitefish. This camp was over thirty miles offshore on the Pack Ice. If the Earth has anywhere more remote, I do not want the experience. Next stop, the gulags of Siberia. Maybe that was the answer for me. I just couldn't seem to get it right in the outside world.

As if in response to my needs, fortune smiled on me—I was allowed to stay in camp for twelve weeks this time.

The cook was an old scoundrel named Terry. In personality, he was as close to Long John Silver as anyone I've ever encountered—someone you hated to love, but did anyway. Shortly after I settled into the new camp, Terry ran off his night cook for doing drugs on the job. Consequently, there was an employment opportunity in the kitchen. So he threw out the statement, "Bob, I think you might have the smarts to be able to handle the job."

My only qualification for the job was my ability to open a can of stew—provided the can opener wasn't too sophisticated. But

Terry was a consummate manipulator, and somehow he knew just what to say to get me going. He challenged me.

Of course, I thought. *Told you. Cream rises to the top.*

So the druggy shipped out; they brought in a new camp attendant to replace me, and I became night cook, which meant that I was also the baker. For anyone who doesn't know, cooking requires smarts—lots of smarts.

Terry was from Australia or New Zealand, a master chef who had apprenticed at London's Savoy Hotel. He was completely overqualified to be a rig cook. He was also a borderline functioning alcoholic. In actual age he could have been anywhere from fifty to sixty-five years old, but he had the mentality and the sex-drive of a fifteen-year-old. He had an Errol Flynn mustache and a good head of hair (I think he dyed it). The ladies—young ones—and booze were his passions. His drinking, compounded by his extracurricular screwing, had dissolved his marriage.

The silly old bugger was a handful whenever we were in Edmonton. He invariably hooked up with losers, young chicks not far from prostitution, druggies. He was always ready to scrap, usually for imagined slights and usually with much younger and larger men. I played the role of peacemaker. If you can imagine. Eventually we started going our separate ways when we were in the city. I just couldn't take the hassle.

When sober, Terry was always smiling. He was a very demanding boss, but God he could do wondrous things in the kitchen. I soaked up every cooking lesson he gave me. On the average night I baked ten fruit pies, ten cream pies, angel-food cakes, a couple of cookie-pan-sized trays of brownies, six loaves of bread, four dozen buns (they were always right out of the oven for the crew change—that was a little touch of *my* marketing instincts there), as well as supper for the guys just getting off the night shift. When I had a spare moment, I baked cookies. A trick Terry taught me was to mix six-dozen batches of basic cookie batter each time, then divide that up and refrigerate the excess. Then all I had to do was pull out the dough and add chocolate chips to one batch, coconut to another, raisins to the next, and white chocolate chips to last. This saved a bunch of time. Every night Terry taught me some new skill—cream puffs, doughnuts, French pastries (had to be folded gently and repeatedly to achieve that layered effect). Terry was never so happy as when he was teaching an apt student. And things come easy to me; I'm a lucky guy.

I found out that the guys on the rig, mostly young guys, were junk-food gourmets. I gave them what they wanted—pizza, milk shakes, grilled-cheese sandwiches, hamburgers, hot dogs—and they loved it. We were in big demand, Terry and I; we went the extra yard, and it was appreciated. The highlights of the day were the meals, and we tried not to disappoint. As the cooks go, so goes the camp.

I finished the season with Terry. I also worked part of the next season. This was a good period of my life.

The next time I went back to Edmonton, I had over thirty-five hundred dollars in the bank, plus five hundred dollars of walking-around money. Scared as hell, I moved into the Sally Anne Hostel. No booze allowed in here. Went to the Al-anon Club for alcoholics, two or three AA meetings a week. I was sick and tired of being sick.

The highlight of the week was Saturday night and the singles dance. I had a tremendous success rate at these functions. While I was making my list and checking it twice—my list of the gals I wanted to spend more time with (and screw)—I let these ladies know that I thought drinking was dumb and that I was having too much fun without it. Later, after eleven o'clock, the list shortened. Most of the male competition had already sailed off to oblivion, and I closed in for the score.

I met a woman who was older by ten years—make that ten long, Jack-Benny-type years—and we hit it off. We started dating regularly. After a while we decided to live together, no commitment. It was a physical thing, convenient for both of us, like Mrs. Robinson in *The Graduate*. She screwed around when I was out of town. So what.

Through her I met a wonderful family, people who were to help me a lot. Marg, Les, and their son Bill became friends extraordinaire. In fact, I eventually left the relationship with Mrs. Robinson and moved in with the three of them. Of course, I continued hitting the singles dances, and eventually met my future wife Pat at one. But I'm getting ahead of the story. Patience is a virtue, Bottlehopper. For now, I was still slipping and sliding, two steps forward, one step back. But, thank God, the forward steps were getting bigger, the backward ones smaller.

You are a lucky guy, Bob...

Terry hated Englishmen with a Passion. "Pommy faggot bastards, to a man," he growled many times. He was trouble personified—an accident looking for a place to occur and, if it didn't, he wasn't above starting something. I asked him what the hell he was doing in the middle of nowhere with his skills. Talk about overqualified.

"Bloody temper, booze, and women," he said.

His temper was uncontrollable when he was drinking. So was his appetite for women, especially men's wives—and their daughters if they were close to legal age.

The Savoy in London where he apprenticed, five-star hotels in the Caribbean—all big-paying jobs that he lost due to booze, fighting, or sexual indiscretions. He told a story about a hotel owner who really was a bit much with his hands-on inspections. He would lift the lids of the staff toilets and never find them clean enough. "I figured I'd set the bloody bastard right," he said.

"I had the lad clean the toilets exceptionally well. Then I took a large dollop of Hershey's liquid syrup and smeared it under the toilet seat. During the kitchen inspection, Mr. Toilet-Fetish lifted the seat and exclaimed, "What is this!'"

After carefully inspecting the dark-colored stain, Terry said, "Looks like shit." Then he reached down and put some on his finger, tasted it, and then replied, "Yep, it bloody well is shit!" Another job in another hotel.

Perhaps, like Bob, Terry only found it possible to function in a booze-free environment like the Arctic.

When he came back to camp, he always brought a couple of bottles to help him over the rough spots—valium (the blue pills, ten milligrams) and librium capsules (the green and white ones, twenty-five milligrams) to smooth out the first couple of days.

No matter, though, when we hit town Terry immediately broke loose and started living up to the outdated reputation of Edmonton. The City of Champions started out as a fur trading post for the Hudson Bay Company. The natives called it Fort Whoop-up. Rotgut whiskey for pelts. The frontier was always a heyday for Ethyl A. For the men who built the Erie Canal, a day's pay was one dollar and one quart of whiskey—dispensed in four-ounce shots starting at six in the morning. The Winchester didn't win the west—Jim Beam and Jack Daniels did.

Terry always ordered too much food, especially Chinese. Naturally my money was no good. I made him at least let me pay for the tip. He's a man I would trust to protect my back, drunk or sober.

Once I set him up with a blind date, a thirty-five-year-old divorcee who was more than I could handle in the sack. But Terry was disappointed. She was far too old. He dumped her and set off for a seedier part of town to find something younger and much more trouble. Black eyes, getting rolled, ending up in jail—these were normal occurrences every trip out. The silly old man couldn't keep it in his pants.

I remained sober a couple of times by out-and-out lying. I had to stop returning his phone calls—at first four a day, then two, then none.

We had little in common as I continued in my sober life. You get to a point that you're just not going forward anymore.

I hope Terry found Viagra and a good nursing home to terrorize. That's the way I want to remember him: the purely devilish look in his eyes and the beginnings of an erection in his pants.

Some kids have enormous ears, or big feet. Terry had oversized, powerful hands. To see him do the magic of carving delicate flowers or decorating a cake with those carpenter's hands was amazing. He could carve flowers out of an apple, tint them with food coloring, then dip them in lemon juice to preserve their virginal blush.

He always said, "Bob, you have way too much smarts to waste your life hiding out in the Arctic camps."

Transitions

The pace of my life accelerated when I met Marg, Les, and Bill Milligan. Suddenly I had decent people who really believed in me. In spite of the fact that I was usually chasing around with Terry in those days, they could see that he was a dirty old man and I was... well, for some reason they thought I was something different. Marg told me that I should stop feeling responsible for Terry, stop bailing him out of jail, stop lending him money after one of his loose Lolitas had robbed him.

Margie and her moral values also got me to terminate my relationship with Mrs. Robinson, the "Dragon Lady." Sleeping around while I was working in the Arctic did not meet with Marg's high moral values.

"Bob, you don't need that kind of relationship. There's a bed in the basement. I want you to move in with us."

They had a better opinion of me than I myself did. They offered support and confidence when I needed it most. God, I loved these folks. Imagine—wanting an old drunk rounder like me to move into their home!

I don't know how to convey the importance of Margie to my continuing recovery, to my life. A word of encouragement here, solid advice there, and always unwavering faith in my future success. Faith in me. Her door was always unlocked and the coffee pot was always full. You just yelled hello, walked in, poured a cup, and gravitated towards her.

She was the neighborhood matriarch. She collected people— strays like me and young people with problems who would come to her for advice and love, and she gave both abundantly. Sometimes she had us doing ceramics. She had the whole set-up, kiln and all.

Do you know the proverb "I wept because I had no shoes, then I met a man who had no feet"? It fits Marg's situation perfectly. The old woman was living with the tragic effects of diabetes that had gone undiagnosed for too long. She had almost no circulation in her extremities. When I met her, she had already lost one leg. During the time I lived with her she went through three amputations, each one higher up on her only remaining leg. She often spent weekdays in the hospital and came home on weekends. Her amputations didn't heal.

Margie was rotund. One tends to get that way sitting in a wheelchair. Besides that, she yielded to her sweet tooth regularly, cheating on her diabetic diet. "What else can they cut off?" she reasoned.

Living there was like living with a saint. You'd come home and someone else would be leaving. Maybe it would be some young woman hugging her and saying, "Thanks I feel better now."

"Everything will work out," Margie would say. "You'll see. You're strong enough to cope. Let's have coffee on Monday. I'll meet you in the hospital cafe at ten."

Later Margie would say, "I met her a few days ago. I feel sorry for her. Her husband's in the burn unit with second and third degree damage to over fifty percent of his body. She has a long row to hoe."

Meanwhile, Marg's surgeons were fighting to leave enough material to support a prosthesis.

She believed in me. She knew that I deserved to be successful. When I was feeling down, I used to go in there and talk to her, tell her my problems, get inspired, regain my objectivity, and then suddenly realize that I'd been boo-hooing to a woman who had lost both of her legs. Then I'd go outside and give myself a tune-up from the neck up.

Good thing I still had the ability to kick myself in the rear end.

The time frame would be early 1979. I had some self-respect back, and I had support from the Milligan family. Working in the high Arctic was okay, but it was a lonely life. My true vocation was sales, always had been. So I decided to try to go back to work.

I needed to see if I could function sober.

I took and passed the pre-licensing course for my real estate license. I interviewed with several builders and chose the one who had built Marg and Les's home. I bought an eight-year-old Mercury Comet for fifteen hundred dollars—presentable, not presumptuous. Suddenly things were falling together.

Could I escape my own past? That was the anxious question in the back of my mind. For example, I had a criminal record. Not much of a record, I admit, but ten years before—as you recall—I had assaulted a police vehicle in Vancouver. I had committed the crime of "public mischief."

In Canada realtors are licensed by the government. One of the main criteria for acceptance is a clean record.

As I was filling out the application to begin my new career, I reached the line that asked if I had any criminal convictions. And I hesitated. I talked it over with my sales manager. His advice: "Just leave that part of the application blank."

"But they can run a make on me pretty quick."

"They'll never find out about a chickenshit public mischief charge," he said. "Not from a hick province like BC."

I had a feeling that he was giving me bad advice. Mom always used to say, "Tell the truth, Bobby. It will set you free." Funny thing about growing older. You keep realizing that those "dumb parents we had" sure said some smart things.

But the sales manager seemed to know the ropes. And I still had some skid-row mentality lurking in my brain. So despite my internal warnings I took his advice.

I started selling homes in August, 1979. From September to December I was the top new-home salesperson in the company. In January of the new year, I met Pat.

In other words, as is appropriate, before I was worthy of her. I had to begin my ascent—my self-created ascent to respectability and success. When Pat appeared, I received the component that had been missing for so many years—someone to talk to and love and share my success with. I was already simmering; Pat supplied the fuel that turned my career into a full rolling boil.

The date was January 8. I was prowling the singles scene, looking for my first encounter of the sexual kind to ring in the new year. Making my list, checking it twice. Bobby's going to get lucky tonight. All I wanted was an oil change and a lube job. No strings, please.

But whoever came up with the phrase "the fickle finger of fate" needs to be given credit.

I met a lady named Pat, danced with her. She made the short list—even though she told me that she was definitely not interested in a relationship, sexual or otherwise. She was still recovering from the loss of her husband two years before. The mind-set was, "Who needs another man? I just planted one!"

Still I kept asking open-ended questions, gathering information, using my listening skills. In my head were the words of The Bard: "Methinks the lady doth protest too much." The flesh is weak, I knew, and I was smooth. Scary smooth. We went for coffee after the dance, got it going pretty good in the car, and then drove our separate cars to her home.

I didn't get to the promised land that night. Close, but no cigar.

Afterwards, I decided not to phone her back.

It wasn't like me to turn down a sure thing—which I knew our next encounter would be—but I still had some vestiges of conscience. Emotionally, she was easy pickings. She certainly didn't need a bastard like me messing her up.

And she was so respectable-nice that she scared me.

But stupid Cupid was picking on me. A few days later, some other guy named Bob left a message on Pat's answering machine, and she assumed it was me. (She wished it was me. Hell I could even jive.) I'd given her one of my cards, so she phoned.

I was out. Poor Les got his lips ripped off because I'd waited too long to call her. Yikes, she was a feisty little thing!

I agreed to drop over Thursday night after volleyball. Shortly after my arrival, she raped me—with little foreplay, I might add. Repeatedly. All night long she continued. At dawn she finally she let me go home. I slept like the dead and woke up smiling, with an erection.

This lady wanted to play ball with me! *Touché*! Fortunately it was Friday—my day off. I was sex-hausted.

As agreed, I called Pat at suppertime, and we went to a hotel and did it all night again. As we walked out of the hotel arm in arm at five in the morning, I asked Pat what she wanted to do the next night. She said, "The same thing we did tonight."

"I'm kind of short of cash."

"Don't worry," she said as she hugged my arm to her breast. "We'll use my Visa."

This woman definitely had a healthy attitude towards sex. My special purpose was aching from the exertion. But what did Lombardi say about playing with the small hurts?

We were both gamers. We both came to play. And it didn't take the brain of a nuclear physicist to realize that we both had incredible needs.

The room cost a hundred and twenty-five dollars, and it had a jetted spa. This enabled us to re-play the Battle of the Atlantic. I was the dreaded U-boat and used my trusty torpedo to sink the poor defenseless merchant ship. It was a dangerous mission; lucky thing we didn't both drown.

On the occasions when we came up for air, the Bottlehopper made a profound discovery. He enjoyed Pat's company when they were out of bed, too.

We shared stories about growing up. I told her about the Bay. Pat told me about her summers in Banff. She used to sell vanilla extract to the Indians so that they would let her ride their horses. She once owned a sling-shot made from a hand-picked maple branch, just like me. She'd plunked street lights with it in Banff, just as I had in the Royal City.

The one story that made me melt was about Pat and the gophers. Pat's dad was a golfer, but he was also salesman who traveled a lot and so left his clubs at home unsupervised. She used to borrow a couple of the wooden-shafted irons. Then she and her friends would ride like Amazons, full-speed bareback through the alpine meadows, using their trusty nine-irons to lop the heads off gophers. Definitely my kind of girl. The kind of girl I would introduce to my mom.

We laughed, we sang, we made love. Long-dormant feelings of caring and sharing surfaced. Bottlehopper's mind-set was to run like hell.

But a little voice was soon to be quietly screaming—go for it. Shoot the bundle.

A week went by and Pat said, "Why don't you move in and we'll save the cost of hotel rooms?"

"No way. It's too soon. What about the kids?"

"I am not asking you to live with *them*. I'm asking you to live with *me*."

"What about your brothers, the rest of your family?" Pat had lots of family in Edmonton. She was a native daughter.

"Screw them. I'm free, female, and nearly forty. I'll do what I please. Only what the kids think is important to me. I've already talked to them, and they think it's great."

I was scared stiff.

I told her that I very rarely drank. She didn't drink, either. I told her that I thought that I had an allergy to the stuff. Never really fessed-up to being a chronic alcoholic, though. Not right away. I really didn't want to rock the boat.

I was able to hold off for a month before I moved in.

My little head had a lot to do with the decision. We were totally awesome in bed. But the other part. The scary part was developing at warp speed.

I had checks and balances in place; I told myself that either of us could pull the plug at any time. Just friends! Just like Gail "We'll Sing In The Sunshine" Garnett. "I'll sing to you each morning, I'll kiss you every night... then I'll be on my way." Yeah, sure, Bob. Admit it now or admit it later, you're hooked—hooked, my boy.

Because I worked the show home till eight at night, I couldn't visit Margie at the hospital until after visiting hours. We had her doctor's permission for my late visits, but the security guards harassed me every time.

One particular night the guard was a new face. Very officious. A boy in a uniform. (If we ever give some of these guys guns, we're doomed.) He asked me who was I going to see.

I told him I was going to see my suffering mother.

He asked for my ID. He studied the paper carefully, and then he looked me in the eye. He wanted to know why my last name was different from my mother's.

"I'm a bastard," I said. "I'm her illegitimate son."

He blushed, and he let me in.

When I told the story to Marg, we were hysterical. Forever and after, my nomer was Bob, the illegitimate son.

My relationship with Pat kept blossoming into a kind of love that neither of us had experienced before.

We played racquetball; she played unbelievably well. Pat got frustrated, though, not only because I'm a gifted player, but also because I'm ambidextrous. When I have to play left-handed, I don't miss a beat. In retaliation she made me play without shoes. Then she made me play without my glasses. Her final revenge, the most female of all, was chemical warfare—Pat let one rip.

"Whoops, sorry. That was *on accident*, as Tricia would say."

Tricia was Pat's nine-year-old.

"Yeah, right. I suppose Delilah told Samson she only meant to give him a trim."

So she defeated me with tears of laughter, compounded by the aroma. What ever happened to the Geneva Convention? All's fair in love and racquetball.

Did I say *"love?"*

When I first moved in with Pat, my estate was meager. I had four pairs of underwear and four pairs of socks.

The first few times we got into the shower together, I wore my socks and undies. I washed them and afterwards hung them up to dry. This was normal behavior for me, a street skill. Eventually Pat told me about the washer, the dryer, the dirty-clothes basket, and the magical way that clean clothes would reappear in my bedroom drawer.

We still get a good laugh after all these years.

My haberdasher was still the Sally Anne. I also afforded the Army and Navy Boutique. Basically, I really enjoyed saving the money.

The clothes were used but they weren't shabby. My appearance at work was very respectable.

I had a lot of difficulty to deal with at work. Enormous challenges. I was a new-home salesman, and the country was mired in a recession. During my first two years, three builders went into liquidation. When they went, I lost a lot of money. In those days, we got paid only after the home that we'd sold was built. If the company went tits up, we got what the seagull left on the rock: doodley-squat. The insecurity was a serenity-tester.

But ask me if I cared. I kept going. The glass was always half-full in those days.

Interest rates soared to the twenty-percent range. The early eighties were tough economic times. But my work ethic and my fierce desire to succeed kept me going. I made sales. Screw the recession— people needed homes! The glass is always half full, I tell you!

In fact, though, I was having difficulty getting paid. By the time I met Pat my nest-egg was pretty well gone.

Pat said, "Tell them you want a thirty-five hundred dollar advance every month on the money they owe you." She knew that big-hitters like me could demand special treatment; I wasn't so sure. In fact, I was afraid to ask. Despite my lack of confidence, though, I took her advice.

Surprise, surprise. Ask and ye shall receive, Bob.

With my first check, I bought Margie a new remote-controlled color television. She was delighted. She couldn't have been happier if I'd handed her a million dollars—so she said. Of course, I wasn't worth a million dollars.

Patience, Bottlehopper. Good things happen to good people.

And then my little white lie on the application form caught up with me. I was summoned to appear before a disciplinary committee to explain my omission of the public mischief charge. When you're summoned by the auspices of "The Superintendent of Insurance," you are in serious trouble.

I decided not to hire a lawyer but just to go in there and face the issue head-on. You do the crime, you do the time. Sure, I'd been given bad advice. But I'd known what I was doing. By not answering the question, I had lied.

When I appeared before the committee, I discovered that my former manager had written a letter on my behalf. In the letter, he took responsibility for having misled me. I got off with a short suspension—one month, virtually a slap on the wrist. I was lucky.

Through small blessings like this I was recovering my faith in human nature. And I was growing in my sobriety

Pat and I were married on December 11, 1982 in Margie and Les's living room. Margie was still not well, and the brutally cold Alberta winters made it difficult for her to get out. We had an intimate ceremony in the living room of our wonderful friends. The reception was at the community center, and it went super. Lots of mutual friends and Pat's family. My two nieces Doris and Audrey flew to Edmonton from the coast. My son was allowed to attend.

I was a married man, happier than I can ever remember, and looking forward to sharing the future with the love of my life at my side. I could barely believe in all these blessings. I said thanks every night. And in the morning I asked for help facing the challenges ahead. Pat knew my story. I got completely honest before the wedding. She knew everything. She had accepted my alcoholism. But every day I still had the feeling that I was driving around with a case of dynamite under the front seat of the car.

In terms of my alcoholism I was very afraid. (Sometimes fear is good.) But time enabled me to grow in my sobriety, and our marriage flourished. Stick by stick, I moved the explosives to the trunk of the car. Then, eventually, stick by stick, I moved them into the safety of my garage. But if something didn't go right at work, or if a deal would flip, I'd imagine feeling that fucking dynamite under there. Definitely time to get to an AA meeting.

That year I was one of the top ten salespeople in the city.

Good Things Happen to Good People

One evening I answered the phone and a voice said, "It's me."

The voice was quivery and decrepit, but also strong and authoritative. "I'll be at the bus depot on Friday, June 6, at 3:00 p.m. Be there to pick me up. Good-by."

"Whoa, whoa," I said. "Who is this?"

"It's Annis," was her snippy reply.

"Hold on a minute. I'll get Pat."

Of course, I'd only been sober for a few years and I was still easily confused. But I'd never heard of an old biddy named Annis before.

Pat took the phone, wrote down the bus information, then hung up. Enter Annis, stage right.

"That was my great-cousin. I'm the only one in the family she talks to anymore. My mom used to call her the nitwit cousin. She lives in Wetaskiwin, a small town, just outside Edmonton. She's eighty-four and quite an eccentric. Usually I phone her from work—that's why you don't know about her."

"Good thing. I thought I'd messed up my marbles."

"No, you're okay. Annis is my mother's cousin. She was a spinster until she was almost fifty, then she married a retired policeman twenty years her senior. I always keep her up to date on all the happenings with my aunts and uncles and cousins." Pat, it turned out, was the only one in the extended family with whom she chose to communicate.

Annis swooped into my life on June 6. The anniversary of Operation Overlord, the Allied invasion of mainland Europe. She entered the house like an occupying army, with all the confidence and logistics of Eisenhower. I must have sensed what was coming because I felt some trepidation as I drove to the bus station to fetch her.

And there she was—short and dumpy, with a lack-of-calcium hump in her back. Her hair was cut short with lots of black mixed in with the gray. The black was shockingly dark, and as I came to know Annis over time, I watched the black shift to different parts of her hair, sometimes spreading outwards from a gray center like a Friar Tuck haircut. Her upper lip sported a rather obvious mustache. The eyes were dark and lively behind her wire-rim glasses. She stood there and blinked, a bit like Mr. Magoo. I could tell she had a few trepidations about this encounter herself.

I walked up to her smiling boldly. And she smiled and, my goodness—her smile just burst forth, lighting up the whole interior of the bus depot.

I could see two things right away. First, that she was in control—I should say, in total command—of her senses. Second, that she was truly a free spirit. Her firm handshake and no-nonsense approach to things was fine with me. We became instant news, laughing and trading stories all the way home from the bus depot. Pat was at work, so the old girl and I shared some special time alone. Must have drunk three pots of tea before Pat arrived. It was *Arsenic and Old Lace*.

She was her own person, a bona fide eccentric. Every winter, she took night classes—foreign languages, electrical repair, wood finishing. At age eighty-four she passed a carpentry course and then used her skill saw and all to add a wall inside her house. Drywall, mudding, sanding, and painting—Annis did the works.

She was feisty, all four-foot-seven-inches of her, and full of a devilish sense of humor. She had fought with every member of the family and hadn't spoken with most of them in forty years. That's why she needed Pat as the conduit for family information. So when Annis came to town on one of her infrequent visits— she lived about an hour's drive outside Edmonton—she always called Pat.

We liked Annis so much that Pat and I swore not to get lured into any of the family beefs that might pass back and forth along that conduit. We worked hard to preserve our privileged status. Pat had an extra motivation—Annis could have passed as a clone of Pat's own mother. From pictures of Ruth, Pat's mom, I could see the amazing likeness.

One piece of family news that Pat had passed on to Annis happened to be about us. Annis knew that we had adopted Meg into the household. Meg was the mother of Pat's first husband, the grandmother of Pat's two children.

We helped Meg immigrate to Canada from the tough side of town in Glasgow, Scotland. We wanted her to spend this part of her life enjoying her grandchildren as they grew up.

Margaret Teresa Fitzsimmons—Grans, as we affectionately called her—epitomized the kindly Scottish matriarch. She was gentle and reserved, but she packed a lot of punch. She had a sharp sense of humor and a dogged, nose-to-the-grindstone attitude. A true survivor.

Born with a hole in her heart, she wasn't expected to live. At age twelve, she was sent home by the doctors to die. But miraculously her heart healed itself, and she went on to outlive her seven brothers and sisters and her alcoholic Andy Capp-clone husband.

She always spoke of him as "the old boy."

Sadly, she also outlived her only son, Frank—Pat's first husband. Many times while she was living with us she said the words, "Parents should not have to bury their children."

She had lived her adult life in Glasgow's slums. She had been widowed for sixteen years by the time I met her. Margaret Teresa lived with us for the next fifteen years. We took her skiing (she watched), to the Pacific coast, and to Hawaii half a dozen times. One swell old gal. Margaret was happier with us than she had ever been. She told me this many times, and she thanked Pat and me for inviting her to Canada.

She passed away in 1997, three days short of her eighty-third birthday. I delivered the eulogy. There were few dry eyes. Mine were as damp as hell. So long, Margaret Teresa—we love you and miss you. God speed, old girl.

Even with white hair Meg was still an attractive woman. Her kind face was smile-wrinkled. She'd taught herself to read, to write, and—most important for a Scot, I teased her—do numbers.

She'd had a difficult life in the slums of Glasgow, but she never complained. She was a devout Roman Catholic. I once said to her, "It must be neat now that the priests are doing the services in English."

She muttered, "No! I dinna like it!"

"Do you understand Latin?" I asked.

"No!"

"Then why in the world wouldn't you like to hear the service in English?"

"It's nay right."

Meg took confession every month although I can't imagine what sins she could have confessed. I wonder if I can afford to have her beatified.

I used to kid her about the Catholic church, its stand on birth control *et cetera*. But if I ever get close to the Pearly Gates and find out that the gatekeeper's a Catholic, I know what to say—"I have friends in both places." To me it's no coincidence that our Margaret Teresa and Mother Teresa died almost simultaneously.

But as much as Meg was angelic, Annis was the opposite. It was white and black; peace-keeper and trouble-maker. They both knew about each other, and both were widows. The similarity ended there. From the minute Annis stepped into the house, the two elderly ladies were caught in a geriatric rivalry.

We took them out to dinner many times, and to hockey games. We toured them through the magnificent new convention center, and we rode them on the new subway system that had been built for the Canada Games. We had Meg with us in Hawaii one Christmas and then invited Annis to join us, too. That really put Meg's nose out of joint.

Meg lived with us; she was a household fixture. But we only saw Annis when she decided to let us see her, and then she would just call and arrive. She visited more frequently after I came on the scene. Two free spirits connecting, I guess.

We never went to her house. She invited us several times, but I gave the honest excuse that I worked on weekends. The truth is that I didn't want to cross over into Annis' territory.

At her place we risked getting drawn into a fight. That, of course, would have ended the relationship. I realized how important the news of other members of the family and their lives was to her. Of course the stubborn old girl called Annis would not admit this fact. We never did find out why she was so anti-family. It didn't apply to us, so therefore it was none of our business. I didn't press. She was really spinnier than shit; we kept closer to her by keeping some distance.

Several years later, Annis revealed to us that she had breast cancer. It was a real shock; we thought of her as semi-immortal. Her first surgery was a radical mastectomy. The doctors had to remove the other breast about three months later. Each time, she recuperated at our house for a few days before going home to Wetaskiwin.

About a year later, Pat and I were in San Diego for one of my week-long power-breaks from the hectic work schedule. While we were there, we learned that Annis had been air-ambulanced to University Hospital in Edmonton. We flew back, tossed our suitcases in the car, and drove straight to the University Hospital.

The cancer had spread to her bowels and liver. All they could do was minimize the pain. Pat visited the hospital every day and watched that familiar face as Annis slipped farther away. In one of her lucid moments, she told Pat that I was to be executor of her will and that Pat was the sole beneficiary of her estate. She gave Pat her lawyer's card.

At her request, we called the lawyer. He confirmed that there was indeed a will. We were startled, but we put off thinking about it.

One day I brought Tricia, my stepdaughter, to the hospital to visit the dying old lady. Tricia's natural father had died when she was seven. As a result, she was out of balance with the Grim Reaper. To her, death was a terrible thing, something unnatural and dreadful. But she trusted me enough to come along, and we went up to see Annis. The dear old girl was heavily medicated and unconscious. I held her hand. I told her that Tricia and I were there and that we loved her very much.

The end must have come shortly after we left. When we got back to the house, Pat had already received the call from the hospital. Annis was gone.

I felt like having a drink, only for a second. Long enough to get my chubby cheeks to an AA meeting that night.

I still can't understand why Annis left everything to us. The very idea of it shocked us both. I fully expected a bastard son to show up out of nowhere and claim his rightful inheritance. But there was no trick. She actually had chosen her cousin's daughter, of all people, to entrust with the remains of her life.

Pat's a smart lady and she's got her own idea why. She thinks Annis appreciated what we'd done for Meg, helping her immigrate, keeping the family close. And Annis saw how happy we are. Pat's thinking is very straight-forward. Good people seem to deserve good things.

Whatever the reasons, thank you, Annis, and God speed, old girl. We loved you the way you were.

In fact, our benefactress had already purchased the burial plot and paid for the service. Typical of this very organized lady. Our only job was to honor her final request—no notice in the paper.

She didn't want any of her enemies at the funeral.

The house she owned in Wetaskiwin was packed with antique Canadiana furniture. When you entered the home, you stepped back in time to the nineteen thirties.

We took a few pieces that we liked. Tricia took a seven-piece four-poster bedroom suite. Pat's son filled truckloads. Then Pat's two brothers had their pick. Nieces and nephews, too. Then Tricia and I threw an estate sale that brought in over five thousand dollars. Imagine that kind of money after so much had already been taken by the family. The house was stuffed to overflowing. The first day of the sale was a hoot—we ended up with over three and a half thousand dollars even though our biggest bill was nothing over twenty. When we got home and Pat said, "How did we do?" Tricia and I threw fistfuls of money into the air, covering the kitchen table, Pat, and most of the floor. It was yet another Kodak moment. I bet Annis had a big smile on her face.

When the dust finally settled, we were about a hundred thirty-eight thousand dollars to the good. Good grief! Just under one hundred forty thousand, tax-free.

If Annis didn't like what we were serving for supper, she would call a cab and go downtown to a restaurant. I can see her in the back seat of the cab as it pulled away, looking straight ahead, chin set, just barely visible above the edge of the window. She was a woman who knew what she wanted. Who am I to question her decision?

Now that I'm clean, sober and helping other people in both 12 step programs, AA and NA, I've entered the most fulfilling period of my life. I feel whole, needed, wanted, and happy beyond the customary dreams of the world. We give a lot to assist recovering alcoholics. We bought three new blood-pressure machines and donated them to the Edmonton detox center. We invite recovering alcoholics into our home, feed them, buy them clothes, find them jobs, pay their rent, take them skiing...I have dedicated my remaining years to trying to do good. If someone reaches out for help, I respond. Douglas did that for me, and Terry, and Marg, and Les, and Bill, plus a whole roomful of recovering alcoholics and dedicated counselors in the rehabilitation field. This is the foundation of my sober life. To be able to give unconditionally is a gift from my higher power, whom I choose to call God.

Good stuff. Good place for Bob to be.

I'm not smart enough to think of stuff like that all by myself. It's Pat, I tell you. Pat—my wanna-be groupie wife—is my partner for life. She's one of kindest, gentlest people I have ever met. Not only do I love her, and not only do I like her, but she's also my best friend. And if you live around someone that kind and caring, you can't help but become a more complete person.

We've both done some hell-time here on Earth. Pat's first marriage and mine were less than ideal. My sabbatical on skid row was terrifying. But the pain of life brought its benefits. It brought us this relationship, which is, for us, unique in its total commitment. We can communicate with trust and mutual respect. We tell each other how we feel. Pat gave me her ultimate compliment when she said, "Bob, I can be as silly or as serious with you as I need or want to be, and I know you will still love me."

I'm a lucky guy.

In our relationship the glass is always half full. We confidently expect good things to happen. It's our time. We accept with thanks any good fortune that comes our way. If we were to win a lotto, rest assured that we would do a lot of good with it.

I guess you could say that we did win the lotto. It came from out of left field with no warning—thank goodness. If either of us had seen it coming, we would have messed it up. Especially me. Ignorance is bliss with me. I'm safer if you keep me in the dark.

Tales of Three Children

One of them, is mine. The other two are Pat's. Two of these three children are messed up, and I have to accept the fact that the curse of Ethyl A pollutes the next generation.

In the case of Pat's first husband Frank, for example, the infatuation with Ethyl made him dump his family. Here's how it happened: the doctors told Frank that booze would kill him. So Pat refused to drink with him. In retaliation, Frank found a lady who would.

The doctors' prediction came true after a few years passed— and those years were full of bitterness and rejection for her young son.

Then, after Frank died, Pat let go of her control of the children. Basically, she would come home from work and feed the kids, and then she'd retreat to her room. The downstairs of the house became the children's free domain. Her son took advantage of the situation. He had chicks stay over; he smoked dope, quit school...

Two years later, Bob entered the relationship. Her son sighed and told his mom that he was happy for her. He could be a kid again, he said. Then the household stabilized, and Pat suddenly resumed her role as the ruling matriarch.

That was trouble.

Her son had lost faith in parental controls, and I was the reason they'd returned to bug him. I tried to get him to like me because I loved his mom. No matter what I did, though, things went downhill even faster. Sure, take the car. Here's some money. I'll take care of Pat.

Spare the rod and spoil the child.

My own son has his own resentments. Some may be subliminal. Some resentments are not. I understand. Let's face it—I disappeared for around 10 years.

I can't change anything about the lost years, but I will be happy to share whatever part of his life that he makes available.

During my first summer with Pat, we went together back to British Columbia and the scenes of my previous life. I was allowed to see my son, then twelve. The initial meeting went very well. I explained to him that the alcohol had made me sick.

"I'm really sorry for all the years we missed," I said. "Hell, not one second of that can be changed. We can go forward from here, though, and enjoy as much of each other as we can."

My first wife was okay with *everything* at this time.

My son and I went to Davidson's Pool, a swimming spot in the Alouette River. It was new to him. By his age, I'd been there many times.

You swung out on a rope over the deep river pool, and if you whipped your torso, you could do a great dive. I went first and did a big showboat move. He was suitably impressed. *What do ya know—some grey-haired guy called Dad came out of the blue, and he's a trip.* I made him climb the rocks to a safe place for diving, and I did a jack-knife.

After much coaxing, my prince jumped.

I visited my wife's parents, and they were super. Sincerely glad I was well and alive. But that Christmas we asked if he could come to Hawaii. We were told that his marks weren't good enough. In the spring we tried to fly him to Edmonton for skiing; once again the response was no. Was my first wife experiencing some belated resentments? Later, she started letting him visit. But we got the word, from the other two children. He was told to take me for everything he could.

No sense punishing him for my sins.

But my ex wasn't the cause of anything. It was the Bottlehopper. I was out of balance with both young men, out of balance big time. The problem with my son was the guilt I feel for deserting him. The problem with Pat's son was the fact that I love his mom so much I wanted to bust my chops to get him to like me. Instead I just became an enabler.

Pat's son is a contrary, "a take" person. When he was 18 I hired him to shovel the snow off sidewalks around some critical show homes. He came back reporting success, and he pocketed the dough. It was a lie. Realtors were wading through drifts to get into the homes. That was the pattern of his behavior. When he was nineteen, just before Pat kicked him out for violating every rule of the house, he split. We didn't hear from him for nearly two years.

Pat and I are givers. After he re-emerged, we gave him the down payment for a condominium, plus legal fees and the first year's taxes. We negotiated to get drapes, curtains, and all the appliances included. No strings attached to the gift.

He never invited us over, but so what? The place went into foreclosure—because he pretended that the lawyers wouldn't do anything if he didn't open their letters—but so what? We paid serious money to stop the foreclosure proceedings—but...

I have to really hold back here. Do I have resentments? Yes, but I'm working on them. Mostly, I feel apathy. These days, I wish him no ill. I have come to the realization that I have to be thicker-skinned.

My own prince is less openly abusive, less calculating and mean, and he lives a thousand miles away, so we don't see him that often. He did come all the way from Vancouver to attend my 50th birthday party. But then he behaved like a puke the entire time. He and his girlfriend sneaked out the next morning and left a note saying that they didn't want to disturb us.

When he was 18, I flew him to Edmonton and bought him a car, and of course he picked one that I said was a bad choice. That's typical, I guess. I lent him a year of insurance on the promise that he'd pay me back at fifty dollars a month. On his drive back to Vancouver, though, the new car broke down, and he held me responsible. He made a couple of payments on his paying the insurance promise, then that was it. When I called to ask him about the missing payments, he chewed me out.

He sent me a birthday card the first year I returned, but never another. Forget Father's Day. When Pat would say to him "Your Dad," he would say, "You mean Bob."

Once my step-daughter called him when he was out and said to the person on the phone, "Please ask him to call his sister in Edmonton. Collect." The reply she received was, "He doesn't have a sister in Edmonton." The call was never returned.

When Bob gets screwed, he likes to be kissed. But I have received no smooches from these two young men. Pat feels sorry for me, and I feel sorry for Pat.

Pat's son and his mom get together on his birthday and such. He even sent her a birthday card this year in the mail. I avoid these occasions by choice. Pat doesn't deserve this kind of treatment from her only son.

I send my prince a birthday card and a card at Christmas.

You can call it tough love. We call it self-preservation. Pat, Trish, and I just shake our heads. During times of absolute insanity I stay sober going to AA, by grace of God, with the love of my wife and step-daughter.

Tricia, on the other hand, became the child I didn't deserve. Pat says that she's more like me than I am. She means that as a positive statement, by the way. After all, I do have a few strengths. Still…Imagine someone as off-the-wall as I am—with boobs. That's my girl.

She started working for me when she was twelve years old. Her first job was to clean my show home. I sent her upstairs to vacuum while I made a few phone calls. She should have been finished in about fifteen minutes. An hour later, though, the vacuum was still going. I could hear some loud banging occasionally.

Curious, I hollered up the stairs but couldn't be heard above the howl of the machine. I climbed the stairs. The noise was coming from the bathroom, and the door was ajar. So I walked over and peeked in.

Tricia, fully clothed, was sitting on the throne reading a romance novel. She had the vacuum running in front of her. While I watched, she got to the end of the page, turned the page, banged on the wall a few times, and ran the vacuum cleaner forward and back a little as she buried herself in the next steamy paragraphs.

I burst out laughing. The fact that she added sound effects endeared me to her for all time.

Of course we had our problems with Tricia, too. We had lots of heated words about boys, her schoolwork, boys, our double standards, boys—normal stuff. But she gave us no mean, calculated behavior. We enjoyed Tricia's growing up. And she was right that we had a double standard. So we kept growing up as she did.

Frank's addiction and untimely death turned his son into a bitter unreachable soul—fearful, self-centered, and selfish. He carries a chip on his shoulder the size of a giant sequoia, and he's carried that tree around for twenty years. By now his Hamlet costume has worn pretty thin with us. How does that Eagles tune go—"Get over it?"

My son never saw me drinking. The cross I bear is simply the fact that I was absent. Still, he clearly has all sorts of unresolved feelings and resentments. Perhaps he is unaware of the depth of his anger.

At one point a counselor—my Sensei, the good Doctor Pagliaro—encouraged me to write letters to both of these young men and tell them that they were absolved of any guilt with me. I did that. I told them that my alcoholism was entirely my fault, and so their problems in relationship with me were also entirely my fault. I apologized. Doctor Pagliaro made me rewrite each letter five or six times. The purpose of the exercise was to set all three of us free.

It worked for me.

Not all family members respond to Ethyl's spells with crippling unhappiness. Despite our age differences, Trish and I grew up together. And we loved every minute of it.

It seems to me that you can't be all things to all people. If Warren and Paul have dysfunctional relationships because I was an alcoholic, well then so be it. I've tried my best, and more, with both of them. I've made amends. I've set them free. I can't change one second of the past; all I can do is make a daily commitment to being the best that I can be for today.

Yesterday is gone. Tomorrow is forever ahead of us. Today, I choose to live—one today at a time.

Here's an interesting footnote. I once had the opportunity to show all three children the place where I'd lived in my skid-row period—the flop under the viaduct. Boy, did I get some looks!

I hadn't seen the flop in almost a decade. When I did, I was overcome with happiness just to be alive. For my family to see where I'd lived—the effect was powerful.

We hopped the retaining wall and made it up the path. The rocks to set the trip were still there. Alas, the broom-handles were gone. Tricia said, "It's really neat up here. You could see anyone who's coming up."

The level area under the roof of the concrete flange still had the charcoal smoke-stains on the concrete from the funeral-pyre-sized fire. "Unbelievable," Pat said as she shook her head. "You were completely secluded right here in the heart of the city."

"Where's your stash?" Tricia said.

"See if you can find it."

Everyone looked. In the end, Tricia got the closest to finding the actual hide. I pulled back years of dead grass and opened my vault to daylight by moving a large rock. There was the heel of a bottle of red-devil wine and a half-pint of vodka.

Pat stood off to the side.

I had tears in my eyes.

The boys smashed the two bottles.

Awards Banquet

In early spring of 1986 Pat and I found ourselves in a crowded banquet hall at the posh convention center in downtown Edmonton. The mayor's wife was sitting next to me. We were at the head table—on stage.

My white tux was making me look good, I knew, but inside I felt a bit uncomfortable. I'm a very private person—though you wouldn't know it from the way I act—and I wasn't used to eating under the gaze of eight hundred people.

It was the Sam Awards, the Canada home-building industry's equivalent of the Academy Awards. I was there both to receive awards and to present some. In fact, as co-chairperson of the Sales and Marketing Committee, I had helped organize the whole event.

I was thinking about my speech; my nerves were a little frayed. A wonderful lady, the mayor's wife—but she was a constant talker. The verbal equivalent of a banzai charge. Any minute now I'd be going up to the podium. I was trying to keep my feces together, and this woman was driving me crazy.

"Bet she doesn't get out much," I whispered to Pat. The mayor's wife, and she doesn't get out much? Very funny, Bob.

"You'll do great, Bob," blared the mayor's wife. "Just have a couple of big glasses of wine with the meal. Sort of mellow you out."

Forgive her Lord, she knows not what she says. Fe fie fo fum, duct tape would be fun!

If all alcoholics were tattooed, perhaps we wouldn't have to put up with people who won't leave us alone when we say, "No, thank you." I always wonder if these people are closet alcoholics themselves, because for them it's suspicious or sinister if someone chooses not to imbibe.

Pat is an angel. She suggested that she and "Her Yackedness" may have more in common. Mercifully, we switched seats.

Everyone says that talking in front of an audience is really spooky. It is! However, I relish these adrenaline rushes. I'm the guy who goes down a water slide and ends up in the hospital for three days with a knuckle torn out of the back of my hand. I don't think of it as a death wish; I think of it as nourishing the inner child. Visceral experience gets the old juices flowing, and when the juices flow, you know you're alive. And public speaking is definitely a visceral experience.

Suddenly, I was up to bat. As soon as I stood up, my mind went completely blank.

"Thank you, Mr. Chairman, honored guests. I have always wondered how someone can speak as eloquently as the speakers have tonight. I just wanted to check under the dais to see if there's anything like that gal from the Police Academy movie under here."

I stepped back and took a long look under the podium. Timing is everything. The longer I searched, the more the audience laughed. For effect, I went down on one knee. I waited until the whole room was hysterical—until we were all broadcasting on the same frequency—and then I felt safe enough to let go and do my show.

The audience loved it. I was riding the Zooz, the same Zooz as before, I tell you. But now the Zooz wasn't trapped in my head, pointless and self-directed. By now I'd learned to turn the Zooz outwards and use it for a purpose. I was cooking. I was a dancing fool, a bloody showboat. I finished passing out the awards, then dived for my seat under an avalanche of applause, feeling as if I'd just been electrocuted.

The rest of the evening went great. Bob received personal recognition in sales; our company won the prestigious Builder of the Year Award. I'm a lucky guy. Funny thing—the harder I worked, the luckier I got. I suppose work is the common denominator in any story of success.

For me, though, sobriety was the real cornerstone of success. Fact is, being sober continues to serve as the single most important ingredient of everything I do. Without sobriety, wife, family, career, and I disappear. Me first, and probably quickly. This is the harsh reality of my addiction to alcohol—that my only choice is to look death in the eye sober, or to hide from it under the influence. Douglas's death taught me that lesson.

Now that the speech was over and the pressure was off, I let my attention wander around the room. The place was filled with salespeople, a lot of them rookies just as I had been only a few frantically busy years before. Now I was up at the head table, enduring the honor of sitting next to the mayor's wife. How did it happen? The pace of my career was moving so fast that I'd hardly had time to ask myself that question.

It began, of course, with the hunt and the chase—I knew how to sell homes. In fact, I was coming off a peak career year with a Calgary-based builder when two salesmen who worked for a rival company approached me in person. They wanted to take me to lunch.

Of course they really wanted to offer me a job. That's how these things were done: secretly. If the builder was a solid company—and this one was—the principals did not want to be seen poaching on another company's staff. Instead, they sent intermediaries to test the water, to see if the prospect was interested. The entire process was James Bondian.

It stands to reason that if you're good at what you do, you should be getting job offers. I had already passed up several other opportunities, and I felt no great urge to shift employers. After all, I was already happy and successful, so why change? The offer would have to be pretty darn lucrative.

Still, my curiosity was aroused, my ego was stoked, and I hated to pass up a free lunch. So I went. And as it turned out, the offer was more challenging than anything I had expected.

My two hosts got to the point while we were still buttering our bread. They needed a sales manager, they said, and was I interested. I said sure, then spent the rest of lunch listening to Ed and Stu talk about their employer.

Manager, I thought to myself. Now that was something new. I'd always been a solo act. But to be responsible for the whole team, responsible for the success of the entire company? I was challenged. I was flattered. Naturally I agreed to talk with the owner. I gave the salesmen one of my cards, suggested that the owner call me at home, and wrote several times that were convenient for me on the back of my business card.

I was familiar with the company. I'd met the principal owner several times at awards banquets like the one tonight, and I'd come away with positive impressions each time. Not only that, but also during the previous year I'd shoveled their snow off the sidewalks. Let me explain: I sold homes that winter in a subdivision where our show home was right next door to theirs, in a new home parade. Their salesperson was pregnant, so every day when I shoveled my walk, I went ahead and shoveled hers, too. Then, after I'd shoveled the competitors' sidewalk, I'd go inside and kick their ass, sales-wise.

Shortly after Ed and Stu laid out the job offer, the principal owner Henry phoned me at home. We had a preliminary discussion and agreed to meet for lunch. As soon as we sat down, he said, "By the way, why did you shovel our walks that winter?"

I gave a small shrug. "Because it needed to be done."

He smiled. It was a truthful answer, but I had the distinct impression that it was also the desired answer. He seemed to think I had the right attitude.

"I have to confess," he said, "I had you shopped by two of my friends."

He meant that his friends had posed as potential home-buyers in order to experience my salesmanship, and sample my presentation and skills.

"I was impressed," he said. "You got both of the parties' names, and you followed up on their questions. In fact, Bob, you almost sold a home to one of my friends!"

We both laughed. My ego loved that. I would have even done it for free.

There were many reasons to take the job. I liked the chemistry between us. Henry was goal-oriented and success-driven just like me. Although his company was a partnership, I knew that Henry was the real driving force. That was to my advantage because I knew that I could trust him to deliver on his promises. I also liked imagining that I'd have more time for my family if I moved into a management position.

But the main attraction of the offer had nothing to do with these—it had to do with the challenge to my personal ambition. He was giving me the opportunity to implement my personal blueprint for success, and then to see the results.

I took the job. By that time I had already earned the practical equivalent of a masters degree in salesmanship. This new job challenge would be my start on a doctoral thesis in sales and marketing.

Management is a different gig from the serendipity-prone life of a salesperson. It stands to reason that the best athletes do not necessarily make the best coaches. In the same way, there's no reason to suppose that a salesperson would necessarily make a good manager. In management, the skills of the hunt and the chase are worse than useless, and yet the business community seems totally unaware of this obvious fact. Business generally rewards excellence in sales by moving its best into senior management positions. Usually, this is a big mistake.

But I was sure I could adapt.

The first nine months on the job were a hectic blur. Almost as soon as I came on board, I lost over half of my guaranteed sales volume. My two top salesmen moved to other opportunities in the industry. They were kind enough to invite me to meet them at one of their homes to break the news. In fact, they were gentlemen about the whole thing, and I was friendly and understanding. Inside, though, I was frantic. This was Ed and Stu—the two guys who had talked me into moving to the company in the first place.

Next I had to face the fact that the company was frugal to a fault. I had come, loaded with successful sales techniques and ready to rewrite the book of proper management of an over-achieving sales team. The company was a major player, moving into the big leagues now. We needed to maintain a presence through advertising—newspaper ads, at least. But the two owners were as tight as steel drums. I had almost no advertising budget. Despite the adage "you have to spend some to make some," it was like pulling teeth to get even the most necessary marketing funds.

So a major challenge of this, my first management job was to improvise around the owners' blind spot. I took several courses at the university on advertising. I read all sorts of books on the subject, highlighted the relevant information, and passed them on to Henry for his perusal. The books showed that we needed a new strategy in order to maintain and increase our market share; it's a fundamental fact of the growth curve. I told the owners that we were being beaten to the punch by other builders. I favored subdivisions where all the builders contributed to a mutual advertising budget. Whatever it took, I did.

I hired two new salespeople and went to work on them like Vince Lombardi himself. Always a voracious reader, I devoured books on management. The phylum Porifera has nothing in its classification that can sponge up more information than the

Bottlehopper. I searched everywhere for ideas that would turn negatives into positives for my team. I taught myself cutting-edge sales and closing techniques, and we implemented them.

Oddly enough, my sojourn on the skids made me a better sales-person and manager. Certainly on Skid Road I'd learned to sur-vive in a hostile, competitive environment. The business world is also a competitive environment that requires some of the same survival skills—especially in sales and marketing.

My skid-road years also gave me some solid experience in hu-man nature at its worst. I relied on this training when it came to hiring and working with salespeople. I listened, observed, asked open-ended questions, and looked for desired qualities and po-tential character flaws. To assess candidates, I used the Ben Franklin technique—reasons to, reasons not to. With the experi-enced staff, I tried to isolate and weed out bad habits as fast as possible—although, for some reason, the ability to change is not a strength in most salespersons. The raw recruits were a chal-lenge as well, but I was able to challenge, teach, and help most of them to become superb salespersons.

Incredibly, my team and I sold sixty-five homes in my first nine months.

I managed the top salesperson in Edmonton for 3 years. Sev-eral others made the top ten. I trained the runner-up rookie-of-the-year five times. Then we won the "Builder of the Year" award, the Oscar of the Edmonton Home Builders Association.

My first full year we built one hundred and eighteen homes. The second full year we built over one hundred fifty homes. As success dawned for the company, I began casting a large shadow in the industry. At builder meetings, people sought my opinions. When I talked, others listened, but I kept fairly tight-lipped. Un-less what I had to say pertained to the common good, I was mute. That was another trick I'd learned on the streets—to take the cotton from my ears and put it in my mouth.

Good sales techniques are good life techniques.

The noble idea of having more time with the family didn't really work out that well. Certainly I had much more flexibility in my hours but I still worked sixty to seventy hours a week. Pat was on my team. Neither of us wanted to eat dog food in our old age. We took quality time each quarter, and then three weeks or more in Hawaii at Christmas, and we agreed to keep rolling the dice while we were on this winning streak.

Meanwhile, I was friendly and humane with my sales staff, but I found it was essential to set personal boundaries. I rarely socialized with them. When I did, I came early and left early.

Salespeople are infamous for their partying and, as you might remember, I have this slight problem with booze.

The formal part of the awards banquet ended, and none too soon for Pat's tired ears. We excused ourselves from the head table and went to dance. Our company had an employee table elsewhere in the room, and after one dance Pat and I joined them. Lots of my peers come over to wish me congratulations. This was going to be a scene repeated many times over the years to come. I had become a big hitter in the new-home industry.

Before we left that evening, I called Pat over to the window of the elegant convention-center ballroom. "Look down there," I said.

Below us was the old riverbank, the concrete abutments, the industrial area of a huge city. "I used to live down there."

"What do you mean?"

"My hidey-hole. That's where I used to sleep. They built this fancy convention center on the hill right over my old digs."

Pat looked for a moment and said, "Well, congratulations, Bob. You've come a long way."

"Funny, but that's not what I was thinking," I said. "It's not so far away as most people suppose."

Six months later my solid foundation with that company disintegrated under my feet when Henry and I went out for lunch to discuss next year's contract.

Here's what I said: "My position is that, through incredible effort on everyone's part, we have a growing market share. The basic machine is in place. Fine-tuning, a couple of area changes, and perhaps another show home will ensure our continued success. We will continue to gain market share as we continue to expand. But I'm not greedy. I'll be happy with the same contract that I had last year. I'm offering that because I feel it's fair for both of us."

I expected Henry to break out in a perspiration of relief. But the look on his face was not happy.

"Then we have an enormous problem, Bob," he said. "I feel some major changes in your contract are necessary. Here. Read what I propose."

I read his proposal then asked if he was serious. How could he be? After all, I had accomplished nearly impossible growth, and I'd pushed his company into the big time.

He intended to reward excellence by cutting my wages.

I was barely able to control my emotions when I replied, "I'll have to take this home. Digest it. Talk it over with Pat."

Using Pat as an alter-ego was an incredibly useful technique. It always allowed me to call a time out and get away from the situation and strategize.

Pat and I dissected the new contract. In essence, it stunk. To make my one-hundred-thousand-plus with the new contract would be difficult. If I simply repeated my stellar performance of nineteen eighty-six, I would lose significant income.

Basically he was offering me about one-third less money next year. Naturally, he expected the same work commitment, if not more. This was frugality bordering on stupidity. I still shake my head in bewilderment. In those days, I shook my head so much that I actually got a sore neck. It's a wonder my noggin didn't just fall off.

Obviously, the owner didn't think I would walk from the company. Boy, was he ever wrong! Walking was my only alternative. He'd hurt my feelings. I didn't trust him anymore, and so the chemistry was gone. I can't work for someone I don't trust.

Still, this was a new experience for the Bottlehopper—to walk from a hundred-thousand-plus job. To do something as radical as cutting off my own nose. To resign.

But it had to be done.

I have no idea why it feels so good to resign. Thank God for self-esteem.

I stalled the owner until just over a week before we left for Hawaii, and then I handed him my notice. I was a complete gentleman about it; I even offered to work for a couple of weeks after we returned from our vacation.

He was angry. He went red in the face. He stiffened up and sputtered, "This is totally unexpected!"

From the heart my honest reply was, "I can't understand why."

Later I realized that he had just made a colossal blunder in the contract negotiations. In fact, when we went to lunch, he had the alternative contract—the "whoops, what was I thinking?" maneuver—standing by. And I'd known nothing of it. I still have the silver serving tray the company gave me when I left. I still treasure the Gold Cross pen that my sales staff gave me.

I had no idea what would come next, but I wasn't overly worried. At a builders meeting I had let it slip that I was going to be looking for a job in the New Year. I said, "This is in confidence."

That's a powerful phrase—"in confidence." My phone started ringing off the hook before we left. By the time we boarded the plane for Hawaii, I'd already received three excellent offers. My choice of new employer was consummated by a handshake—with the part-owner of the Calgary firm that I had left three years previously—not much over a week after I resigned. I was to be the director of marketing for Homes by Jayman (Edmonton) Ltd.

I was overjoyed to work for Jayman. They were the most forward-thinking company in the business, and they treated their sales staff with respect. Realizing that nothing was built until the sale was consummated, the company believed in training the sales staff, sending them to seminars, setting goals, creating mission statements, finding the critical path, and stretching the envelope. I thought I'd died and gone to heaven.

For this company, Bob had a specific mission—to break into the promised land of one hundred sales within a year and a half. That was my mandate. I even had a budget. We signed the written contract when I returned from the islands.

For the record, we got to one hundred sales in less than a year and never looked back.

It was sort of cute how things worked out after we returned from Hawaii. You remember that I'd agreed to work for Henry a couple of weeks on my return. As promised, I went back to tie up any loose ends, even help train my successor. Henry grabbed me as soon as I walked through the office door while I was still jet-lagged.

"Bob, let's go have coffee. I want to talk to you privately. I haven't slept for a month over the mistake I made with your contract. I checked around with your sales staff and in the industry to find out your worth. We'll tear up the proposed contract, go back to the original one plus these other incentives."

My reply was the same as before. "Pat's my partner. We'll digest this new proposal and decide in a day or so."

I hadn't even considered asking for anything more. Now it was being offered. To walk from a hundred thousand dollars is ballsy; to walk from a hundred fifty thousand is lunacy. But that's what I did.

You remember the handshake, before I left for Hawaii, with the Calgary builder. I adhered to that, and to the fact that my chemistry with Henry was gone. Monkeys and peanuts. *C'est la vie*.

When I faced Henry and turned down his offer, he said to me, "Your predecessor fell on his ass when he left us. Perhaps you will, too."

That was the best thing that he could have said. The gauntlet was thrown. Never mind "thanks for the memories." Thanks for the motivation. I was juiced!

Funny how things turn out. Their top salesperson grew mediocre, and then he left. They never won the builder-of the-year again. Then they split up the partnership and the company vanished.

My star turned supernova. I was going to go into warp speed. No builder has ever had the success we enjoyed. We won builder-of-the year for three consecutive years—an unprecedented achievement. I had four sales staff in the top ten. I was number-one in sales volume for nineteen ninety-one—with over seven million dollars in personal new-home sales. Won the Grand Sam award for sales excellence and for contributions to the industry two years in a row. I have a Lennie Award for being the top salesperson in Canada for Lehndorff subdivisions.

I thank my previous employer for the motivation. More than that, I thank AA and my higher power.

The stress was incredible. Cracks were beginning to show in the old war-horse.

I just sucked it in and kept going.

Success

Success, too, is an intoxicant.

One year, the Bottlehopper made as much money as the president of the United States. The next year he made a tad more, but he almost died in the effort. Was it a fair exchange? I'll probably be asking myself that question till the day I finally croak.

A pay-off like that doesn't come by accident. For me, being a new-home salesperson wasn't a mere job; I embraced it as my true profession. In other words, I was a fulfiller of dreams. It's an enormous responsibility to facilitate the biggest single investment that people make in their lives. I took my clients' needs seriously and totally committed my life to being the best in my field. For me, the clearest sign of success was that forty percent of my sales came from referrals by past customers, people who were totally satisfied.

But the price I paid was dear. Working ten to twelve hours a day seven days a week was tough on me, and especially tough on my loved ones. Pat was great at capturing everything we could from that supply-stream of wealth while it lasted. We both knew it couldn't last forever. In other words, we knew I couldn't keep up the pace indefinitely. But I loved it. After a ten-year sabbatical on skid row—when I was trying to kill myself—now I was ready, willing, and able to catch up. I was driven by the peer recognition, the money, and the sheer momentum of productivity. No time, no time. No time for family. I'm late, I'm late...

Bob, you're in danger again. We know that you're strong like a bull, smart like a tractor, but remember where you came from. For a millisecond, just think.

No time. I'm late...

Homes by Jayman (Edmonton) Ltd. was a family business—father, son, and son-in-law owned 50%. The parent Calgary division owned the other half. I was creating huge success for the company, and that was causing problems. Incredible friction built up around me. The three Edmonton principals were feuding. The father and son used me as a whipping boy, and the son-in-law used me as a buffer between them and him. The politics and family squabbling had no business being carried into the office.

As director of marketing, I had six sales staff and I still worked sales shifts in the show home. I was zooming. Zooz! I endured incredible stress in exchange for the handsome pay. Even so, my pay annoyed the greedy father and son—despite the fact that they expected me to work to the breaking point. And I was happy to work to the breaking point. But the company's internal problems started pushing me past that point into dangerous waters.

I sensed that the old body and spirit couldn't handle this out-of-control pace. But I couldn't see that this success business was driving me right out of my mind. Instead, I stress-managed by eating and put on eighty pounds. Then I became diabetic—a big-time diabetic. Sixty units of insulin a day. Still I kept going. No time for AA. No time to listen to Pat. I'm late. For a very important date.

With Ethyl A.

After ten years and eleven days, I conned myself into a drunk.

Only a couple to help me cope, keep the balls in the air, work things out. Yeah, sure, Bob. We heard this bullshit before. You know you can't shit a bull shitter unless he wants you to.

I knew what I was dealing with. For someone like me there's no guarantee that you can get the genie to go back in the bottle. I am always one drink away from disaster, and I always will be. That's the harsh reality of alcoholism.

But when the beast howls, logic and reason vanish, and I become powerless. Once I begin, no one can stop me. Remember the complete predator, Mr. Hyde—boB, who stomped the femur? God, grant me the serenity...

Unless you're chemically dependent, I don't think you can relate to this insanity. Alcoholic reasoning just can't be explained.

I went to the liquor store and stocked up with a case of mixed bottles—the best brands available. After all, I was a big-hitter businessman. I drove to a hotel and agreed on a price to leave my car for a week. I gave them some crap about going to the coast for a week. Then, with most of the booze safely stashed in my duffel, I took a cab to another hotel. I told the desk that I'd had a tiff with my wife and needed a few days alone. He was not to give my name out to anyone. I rented a room for a week and tipped him twenty dollars. Clearly, no matter what else I may have been saying to myself at the time, this was a planned drunk.

Then I had to phone Pat. Otherwise she would have been worried. God, that was hard. I procrastinated for an hour.

"Hi, babe," I said. "I know I'm late. My head is all screwed up. I need a few days alone."

When she answered, her voice was shaky. "I know you're having a hard time with all this shit at work, but please come home."

I mumbled, "I can't." I am drinking.

"Okay. See you when you can. Love ya a whole bunch."

Usually husbands pull this sort of thing to get a stray piece of tail, but this drunk wasn't about getting laid. With me, planned drunks are about self-destruction—nothing else.

After a couple of days, the Bottlehopper was doing nothing but sitting in a room with the curtains drawn, too fearful to walk down the hall to get a soda for mixer. Too paranoid to go downstairs to eat.

On the third or fourth day, the Bottlehopper woke up out of a drunken stupor to find pizza everywhere. Every mirror was covered in pizza, even the vanity and the bathroom mirrors. Bottlehopper must have been angry with his reflection. It was four in the morning.

Glug.

I started to clean up. No real damage. Just a lot of pizza everywhere. Soapy water worked great. I rinsed and glugged and rinsed and glugged and voila! (Glug.) It was done.

Had to think about moving on. I'd stalled the room cleaners for a couple of days now.

Shit, I burned the damn chair! You're a handy guy, Bob—turn over the cushion.

Got a couple of burns on my chest.

I resolved never again to smoke lying down. Did I hear that some time in the past? Glug. Slow down, asshole, If you want to get out of here, stay ambulatory.

Had to replenish. I remembered that I'd left the reserve stashed in the car at the other hotel, so obviously I was having brief periods of sanity. Glug. I cleaned up in the shower and scraped my face. A splash of after-shave, why not? I decided to slum it and have a drink. Do I prefer the taste of after shave? Yuck, shit. I'd forgotten about the gag reflex. I almost threw up. This was sixty-dollar-a-bottle stuff, not Aqua Velva. After all, I was a success now.

It's still an acquired taste, after-shave—even the expensive stuff.

I blew the scene in style by cab. Hit the liquor store and bought a half-dozen bottles, found a new hotel, and ran the same old con job. After the first bottle, old habits resurface quickly.

After I got settled in, I made a decision to quit my job. So I phoned my boss, the son-in-law, and said, "Hi, boss. I quit. It's been a slice. But I can't function with all this fighting going on in your family." I am also drinking again after ten fucking years sober.

He said, "Sorry, Bob, but I won't let you quit."

"Is there something you don't understand about the words 'I quit?'"

"No. I just won't accept it."

"Just a bloody minute here. This is Canada. I can quit if I want to."

"No, Bob. Take a month. Take six months. Take a year. But you can't quit."

Fuck! It was *déjà vu* all over again. Just like the sergeant on the desk at the police station. I told the boss to get sick, make love to himself, and to shove the job where the sun don't shine. I hung up. Glug! I am a great communicator—what the heck is wrong with these people? Nobody ever listens to a drunk, I guess. Glug. I closed the curtains. That's better. Now I'm safe. Glug. Glug. Glug.

Oblivion!

I ended up in detox. But first into the hospital by ambulance. Emergency. I was having respiratory problems again. I just stopped breathing. Sleep apnea was part of it, and the diabetes. So they needed to stabilize me. I was miserable. I lay there staring at the insanity of my obsession.

I think I'll skip over the details of the flagellation I gave myself. Trust me, I'm a master at it. The main point is that I was safe now. Nothing permanent had gone wrong. Now the guilt would keep me going.

I took three weeks off and then went back into the meat grinder. My boss, who was the company's largest shareholder, told me that he'd talked with the family and that the misery was over. I wouldn't have to endure their squabbling any more. Yeah, sure. People were still at each other's throats. In the end, the company split. The split was a mess, and I was in it up to my ass. I kept going to AA, though. I was sober. I was okay.

That's what I kept telling myself, but it was bullshit. My health was going down the tubes. Diabetes, bronchitis, pneumonia. I was overweight and frustrated. I couldn't cut the stress. My lungs were shot. I was in a massive depression. Putting on the masks like Lon Chaney, Bob withdrew into himself, hiding his feelings. Six months later he went on another binge.

This time he almost died.

My reduced lung function combined with the alcohol to drive carbon dioxide into my blood. In the intensive care unit I stopped breathing and literally left.

When Pat saw me, she said, "Mr. Edwards looks horrible. What's the matter with him?"

"He's looking a lot better," said the doctor. "At least he's breathing now. We had to intubate him." Pat was an emotional wreck.

She and I had a long discussion on one basic point—that this slipping back to drinking couldn't go on because it was killing us both. We resolved that I would go back into treatment at Henwood, a four-week residential program, and try to get it together.

I was two months sober before I went to Henwood. For the first two weeks of the program, we didn't get to go home. Too many patients went missing in action if they got out after only a week.

I was on full medical disability and having serious thoughts about my job. I kept hearing the Beatles singing "money can't buy me love"—and it couldn't buy me the ability to work like that without ruining my health. I completed the course, remained on full medical, and took Pat to Hawaii for two months in the sun. I felt healthy there in the sunshine and the humidity. But when I returned in late January, I had trouble with my lungs again and went back into the hospital.

Bob, you're falling apart. I wanted to work, but my health was failing me. Finally, I got it.

The job was really over.

One of the principals called and wanted me back. I told him that I wasn't well enough to return to work. For once in my life, I put my health first. I was under doctors' care, and I was going to remain there until I got the green light from my medical team.

I'm sad to say that this boss of mine didn't think I was really sick. But my clinical psychologist was a great guy, and he called and convinced the man that I was a living mess. This was Dr. Pagliaro, recommended by detox, and he was a godsend. More than a professional help to me, he became, and still is, a trusted friend. He became my "Sensei," and I became his "Bottlehopper" — our spin on the name Grasshopper from the old TV show Kung Fu. I still possessed a little sense of humor. But I had a long way to go physically, mentally, and spiritually.

There were bad feelings. Debilitating bad feelings. The company had divided, and one side felt I was a traitor when I tried working for the other on a rehabilitation basis. I just couldn't handle the squabbles any more. My new work schedule was suppose to be part-time, but by now you should know how long that lasted. Hell-fire and damnation! I didn't want to leave any money lying on the table. More than that, I wanted to work. I was lost without my job.

But now I was creating waves at home. Pat is the type of person who wakes you up to take a sleeping pill. She called the doctors and ratted me out—my chest, then diabetes, my weight, and now I was faced with a reduced lung capacity. My team of physicians wrote a letter. If I didn't withdraw from the industry immediately, they said, I could and would suffer a fatal attack.

When I notified the insurance company of the decision by my medical team, I was cut off my benefits. That blew me away!

Finally I had to go on full medical disability—May sixteen, nineteen ninety-six. Under duress, I might add. I was angry. Getting put out to pasture at fifty-two is the pits, especially for someone like me. The old war-horse went out with his boots on and his six-guns blazing. My last quarter of working for a living lasted only one month and sixteen days; even so, I achieved over two point three million in that last abbreviated quarter. Good enough for second place in the greater Edmonton area.

It would take me two years to come to terms in some way, any way, with this forced retirement.

University Lecture

We find ourselves at the University of Alberta, in the city of Edmonton. It's mid-October in nineteen ninety-seven A.D.

I like to say the "A.D." When I say it, I think—After Drinking. After Drugs. There are so many negative triggers out there in the media, movies, the television—little messages, sometimes subliminal, that it feels good to get high. That it's necessary to drink just to be socially acceptable. That a party involves people trying to pour drinks down your throat even when you don't want one. Out of self-defense, I use my own positive triggers. It's this recovering alcoholic's way to fight back.

I have come to the University of Alberta at the request of the dean of psychology. He is my Sensei, the same Dr. Pagliaro who helped me climb back out of my last detox experience. I have been seeing him professionally (his profession, not mine) for several years.

The doctor has invited me as "an authority on substance abuse" to talk to his postgraduate students—earnest, inexperienced experts working on masters degrees or doctorates. Substance abuse from my perspective, he feels, will be a big help to his students. Not many who are as successful as I was have gone as far as I did into the abyss. Very few live to tell the story.

We are in a typical classroom setting: too much light and no windows. The burnt-electric-wire smell of ganglia from the twenty or so convoluted brains permeates the air. I'm sweating blood as usual before speaking engagements. I like the rush, though. I've learned that I'm an adrenalin junkie.

Presently the attention of the students is focused on a remarkably good documentary on "Vincent the Vulgar," a day in the life of a skid-row derelict. Afterwards, my goal will be to convince the students of something hard to accept—that I, Mr. Big-Time Bob, was, at one time, Vincent the Vulgar.

How do I convey to these shiny faces in learned places the terrible extent of the chronic phase of my alcoholism? I know inside that I can. After all, I have the equivalent of a doctorate in the subject, with honors. But the key is to do it well and truthfully so that these wonderful folks get a new perspective on the disease.

As I peruse the room, I notice reactions, both verbal and non-verbal. This chronicle of Vincent is holding their attention. Personally, I'd prefer to keep mine elsewhere. When I watch Vincent do what chronic alcoholics do, I feel as though someone is walking over my grave.

Vincent drinks what, and as, I did. He forages for alcohol in all its many forms. He forages like a ruminant on the Serengeti. Some of the elixirs he consumes are conventional; most of them are bizarre. Drug store stuff. The weird elixirs are far more easily boosted.

The hair on my neck has bristled. After all these years I still get a visceral reaction when I see someone drink like that. The aroma of methyl alcohol or vanilla extract still gets a big-time reaction from me.

Mercifully, the pungent aroma of bourbon, rye, and scotch doesn't—the smell of the conventional stuff doesn't bother me. Now that's a pair of ducks flying over Edmonton, for sure. Or could it be simply my body's natural reaction to the fact that I'd kill myself on the conventional stuff now? Now that I can afford to buy it.

When the cost factor doesn't enter the equation for an alcoholic, the results can be scary. Especially for one like boB.

As we watch Vincent slip into yet another drug store, I start calculating how many doubles I could buy right now, if I wanted to, with the money I have in the bank. I'm trying to figure out how to measure that in relationship to my age and the condition of my liver. I give up. Got to hire a constipated mathematician and have him work it out.

Just as sure as shit stinks, I have another drunk in me. Alas, though, I fear that I've used up all of my nine lives of recovery.

What's that? Dost thou think I protest too much? Walk a mile in my shoes, mother-fucker. I have been there, done that and bought the tee-shirt. I earned my bones. That street urchin in the video that was boB. If anyone tried to walk that mile in my boots—methinks a cold glass of water, a pinch in his ass, and he'd be dead.

Vincent is over, and now Dr. Pagliaro is showing a videotape about me.

It's not a documentary; it's just raw tape shot with a camcorder clamped to a tripod. My former boss, Jay, is standing at a podium and pontificating my accomplishments to an assembly of business leaders. He's saying things that I could never, in modesty, say myself. These graduate students are certainly getting his basic message—that I was a big hitter.

I should allude specifically to The Babe pointing into the bleachers and putting the next pitch right there.

It occurs to me that Babe Ruth embodied the point of my coming to speak in this classroom: it ain't over until it's over. And it ain't bragging if you have, in fact, survived.

You can borrow the video, by the way, and watch the whole thing. After Jay gets done with his "Ode To Bob," I get up and tell the Bottlehopper's secrets of success. You'll learn not only how they get the caramel in the caramilk and why the sky is blue, but also how to increase your productivity, set goals, succeed in sales, and manage your financial portfolio. I divulge the rule of seven-point-two in investing. You'll also learn how to lose weight, improve your sex life, firm your breasts and buttocks, enjoy your children, look reality in the eye and deny it, know when to fold them, know when to run, stop taking yourself too seriously, have fun living each day to its fullest, and feel fifteen years younger on the inside where it counts.

Wow.

One of the last of the vanishing breed of true capitalists. And here I am to give a talk as a courtesy. For free.

Actually, I'm doing this for the most selfish reason of all. To help me stay sober. The best way to keep one's sobriety, and to have the best quality of sobriety, is to give it away.

That's a primary reason why AA works.

On the video, Jay is saying, one of the truly greats blah blah salesperson of the year, Grand Sam Award winner two consecutive years blah blah. We could have brought someone in like Anthony Robbins or, or, or, Tom Hopkins and paid him five thousand dollars per day blah blah. We decided to stretch Bob out, expand his career, put him into management. Not only did he continue to make the top ten but also four of his five salespeople did. Bob is one of the truly greats I have had the pleasure of working with...

This kind of an introduction coming from Jay, a demanding driver-bold personality, is an achievement I will treasure for the rest of my life.

If I had known how much he valued my services, I'd have asked for more money.

Finally Bob Edwards is introduced on screen. In the video I'm wearing the exact same clothes that I decided to put on today. I thought it would help the students recognize me. Or perhaps it was my sick attempt at levity. I was thinking—you never can be too sure with a room full of shrinks. Don't want to stretch the collective envelope. Save as much of their gray stuff for afterwards. Hopefully we can get into a symbiotic relationship. Interact.

Because I'm here to drain the swamp.

It's an excellent way to catch alligators.

The room is unnaturally quiet. For me that's a great sign. The students are really into the video presentation. Great body language, taking notes, this is good stuff! Piece of cake, Bob. You got 'em.

On screen I'm waving my arms like a band conductor. Then at the predetermined spot Dr. Pagliaro cuts the video. Mentally, I'm still waving the same baton. I'm stoked. Pitter patter, let's get at her.

The lights come on, and down the aisle walks the reformed drunk. Some of these academics are clapping. Nice to get warm fuzzies. Not that important to me, though. Not any more. I have my self-esteem again. I know my strengths, and they are manifold; I also know my weaknesses, and they are manifolder.

Got to balance the yin and the yang.

I begin by thanking the doctor and thanking the class in advance for giving me a good grade. Then I say, "By the way, Doctor Pagliaro, was there any follow-up on Vincent? How soon after they made that video did he die?"

I thought of the question on the way to the pedestal.

He looks surprised. Then he says, "Just under a year after the documentary was completed."

Amazing. How did I know that Vincent had died?

I say, "I was a witch in a former life. They burned me in Salem. Now I'm a warlock. I've got to warn you that you'd better ask great, challenging questions, interact, take notes, or else bad things could happen."

Fee fie fiddley I oh! Strummin' on my old banjo.

They are straight as arrows. The eye contact is visceral. Great stuff. These students I can work with.

"I knew Vincent was dead. But that was a lucky guess based on my experience and on the condition of his eyes. Vincent had zombie eyes, walking-dead eyes, resigned-to-his-fate eyes, no-fight-left eyes. He had the eyes of a concentration-camp victim.

"Fact is, I'm not a witch or a warlock. The eyes do reveal much. Take a long look into insanity, into Charles Manson's eyes. If some bleeding-heart liberals ever let that dude out, hang onto your hat—that is one sick puppy."

I feel like a young Muhammed Ali, floating like a butterfly, stinging like a bee.

In the video, just when Doctor Pagliaro pushed stop, I had already come up to the podium and received the applause. I was holding up both hands, one of them with the fist closed and the other wide open with a rock in it.

"Which hand is the rock in?" I was saying.

So now I repeat the performance. I raise the open-palmed surface of the left hand to the scholars, then the tightly-closed right. "Which hand is the rock in?" I wait as they look in astonishment. Consensus is achieved. They pick the hand with the rock in it.

It's not a trick.

I can definitely work with these dudes.

"We can cry tears as big as bovine droppings for Vincent," I say. "Or else we can use this time to delve into the psyche of a recovering alcoholic, someone who experienced those same terminal stages of chronic alcoholism and survived. Which would you prefer?"

They're into it now.

"My name is Bob. I'm a palindrome. I like to think in a dual concepts when discussing my chemical dependency. The good guy you see in front of you spells his name capital-bee oh bee. The other spells his name lower case-bee oh capital-bee.

"The problem with lower case-bee is that he's contrary. He spells the name backwards. He uses the vocabulary of the street Quite a disgusting character. Hopefully I will be able to give you some glimpses of him as we proceed in this adventure. The vocabulary of the street is colorful. I apologize in advance for any swearing."

Everyone okay so far? Glancing around the room, maintaining eye contact, got them in the spell of the ZooZ. Bob, you're pretty to watch!

"You're out of your fucking minds if you agree to, or even con- sider, working with alcoholics. From my rock, you'll be dealing with one of the truly baffling, most cunning critters that God ever created. We are consummate liars, manipulators, harborers of realistic and unrealistic fears, self-centered, selfish, angry, moody, and unpredictable. For the sake of your own sanity, when you see one of us coming, run like hell."

I tell them, "Unless you need the dough real bad, stay away."

It works every time. Tell 'em they can't have something, and they want it big time.

"Let's relax for a few moments."

I check with the good doctor. The nonverbal connection is made. I'm such a ham!

"I have no sympathy for Vincent. But I do have empathy. I was Vincent. I would steal your wallet and then help you look for it. It's only by shit house luck or divine interdiction that I am not dead."

Perhaps the devil does take care of his own.

"The bad, lower-case boB and Vincent are a couple of losers who used a system designed to facilitate their addictions. Vincent and I are two peas in the same pod. Fortunately for you, unless you want to do some pro bono psychology, you'll never cross sabers with the Vincents and lower-case boBs of alcoholism.

"If you did, the first priority would be nose plugs. We usually smell disgusting. If we've been drinking vanilla, the pungent smell of shit mixed with an essence of Christmas cake can really make you gag."

I observe noses crinkling.

"Besides, methinks you'll agree that the Vincents and boBs of the world generally lack disposable income to remunerate you for your services. Vincent, the poor sorry soul, doesn't want, and now doesn't need, your expertise."

At least he is at peace.

"The much more sophisticated dudes that you're going to deal with will be much harder cases to crack. The patients who can afford your services will be functioning alcoholics. Perhaps they'll come to you as the result of an ultimatum from an employer, a spouse, a DUI—or it may just be a result of the big scare.

"If you see one coming, run like hell.

"A person like this doesn't want your help. Subliminally, in the initial stages of denial, he really wants you to teach him how to drink normally again."

Any questions?

"Recommend AA and take your fee. Alcoholics Anonymous works best for most. When the patient returns in a more workable mind-set, then you've got a chance—but if the individual isn't totally honest, not much of a chance. That's reality!"

Fe fie fo fum, this is really a lot of fun.

"Run like hell, or you might find out first-hand why those in your profession have such a high suicide rate."

Challenge!

"When they're forced to deal with their addiction, most practicing alcoholics can't tell the truth from a snowstorm. Some will even come to appointments using. When confronted, they will lie.

"Get with the fucking program—it's a war out there. Pills, booze, drugs! The hell of war is casualties. Be like a good general and accept the casualties; minimize the loss of life. Medi-vac the ones with a chance of survival first. Weed out the ones who are blowing sand up your rear.

"Ask them to give a urine sample. Then, when it tests positive, ask them to leave."

I'm thinking, the truth will set you free, Bob. So I launch into it.

"The abuse of alcohol crystallized all of my character defects. It triggered my most unrealistic fears, and it released me from the moral behavior I was brought up to emulate. The result of this phenomenon was the precipitation of a chemically dependent, piss-your-pants, choke-to-death-in-your-own-puke alcoholic. Seizures, DTs, the whole nine yards. I lived in the parallel universe of chemical dependency for ten years and survived.

"After inebriating myself against the vagaries and sheer terror of life, I became an alcoholic. Bob became boB.

"Lower-case boB was a coward. He couldn't cope with the harsh reality of living. He could not, not drink. If he did, withdrawal meant grand and petit mal seizures.

"His—no, alcoholism led me, sometimes slowly, more often quickly, to the complete loss of control of every function of my existence. Bladder control. Wetting myself in a catatonic sleep.

"Alas, only a derelict. Zombie-like, I shuffled my feet forward, urging my boots to clomp on through those monotonous, moldy years. There were no reds, yellows, oranges, or blues. Only lifeless gray. Only surviving the day. Only staying numb.

"I can't tell you whether the world that I chose to live in even existed. It was a universe of half-truths and innuendoes. Raw fear. Failing health. Inability to prowl for money and score drinks from marks. Seizures. More frequent blackouts. The tolerance for alcohol deserting me. A repeat customer in emergency rooms. The inability to judge my intake with any consistency. The inability to secure enough medicine to get through to the next day. Malnutrition. The paralyzing fear of becoming prey rather than the thunder lizard, king of predators. Struggling to survive in my chosen lifestyle.

"The key word is chosen."

There is no good picture of this lifestyle except that which you can create in your mind. Not only was there no "off" switch to the disease but there was also no "off" switch to what it did to my mind. I was trapped in the Zooz.

After the presentation, we interact. I feel that I've done okay. The talk was well received.

The sanctuary of Doctor Pagliaro's office is a den of organized confusion. We hug and shake hands. We spend some time reviewing the presentation. I am relaxed with this man. He has been so important to my recovery.

He tells me that my talk was excellent.

"Bob you really are quite special," he says.

"Gee thanks, Louis. As in special education?"

"Bob," he says, "for goodness' sake, learn to accept a compliment without being flippant."

This Sensei dude is scary. He really knows where I live.

I still have many weaknesses. That's okay, though I'm working hard at being complete. I can laugh at myself now. Can take the blow. I look forward to each day and want the challenges. Hell, I need the challenges to continue growing in my sobriety. I need the challenges to feel alive.

"You know, Sensei," I tell him. "You've come a long way during this time I've been donating to work on you. Quantum leaps, so to speak. But we still have to get your weight and cholesterol levels down, or else you're a no-Sensei guy."

Methinks the good doctor sees all his own defects of character manifested in me. After each session I believe he whispers a silent prayer: "There but for the grace of God..."

Lou shakes his head and smiles, "Bob, you're quite a guy."

The metamorphosis was complete. After all the changes of the larva and pupa, the Bottlehopper emerged. A man who fell asleep and dreamt he was a drunk, and upon awakening didn't know if he were in fact a man dreaming he was an alcoholic or an alcoholic dreaming he was a man.

The profound insanity!

Yesterday and Today

Some folks say, "If I knew then what I know now..." As if they would like to do it all over again. This unbelievably fortunate recovering alcoholic says with conviction, "Once is enough."

I mean it, too.

I feel blessed to have passed this way and survived. And I'm always checking my rear-view mirror to remember where I came from. This may sound corny, but I'm smart enough to say thanks every night for having had the opportunity to be as good as I could that day. In the morning I ask for help to get through the day. Help to do some good. Help with the challenges. Help staying clean and sober for the day.

I have no illusions of saving the world. I'm not that presumptuous. All I want are chances to help, chances to lead by example to the new person, the person who has made a decision to try, the person who has decided to get help for his or her chemical dependency. If I can say or do something to help, it's been a great day.

Where am I today? Well, let's see.

The location is half a block from Kamaole Beach on the Kihei side of Maui. We are here for six months. I have to get out of the Edmonton cold because my lungs can't take the winters. Part of my medical disability.

Five years ago on a fateful Sunday night, almost by fluke, I attended an AA meeting full of Kihei's recovering young American alcoholics. I was startled by the sincerity, the commitment—and the youth!—of these incredible people. This visitor from Edmonton got hooked on the idea of doing some good with these young men and women.

I became involved. As a result, I became unconditionally accepted.

Castle is an out-patient counseling program on Maui. Last year, a dear friend working as a counselor in the Castle program asked me to help six young Hawaiians do the first three steps of the recovery program. What an honor to be asked! Naturally I accepted.

We met twice a week. The oldest in the course was seventeen. The youngest was thirteen.

Children today have a meat-grinder of drugs to choose from. The hell of it is—when you go into the meat-grinder, you get ground up.

From the old stand-bys pot and alcohol to the much more sophisticated batu (ice, crystal meth), heroin, and crack cocaine, sadly, Ethyl A's pantry has so much to choose from.

Today's young people are bigger, smarter, and stronger. Just like today's athletes. The down side to that fact is substance abuse—an international problem of terrible importance. Our young people are killing themselves. The statistics are staggering. I have a finite amount of faith in our young men and women. Empathy, too, for the choices they have to make. For example, when I was their age, all I really had to worry about was making a girl pregnant. Today's youth have the harsh reality of AIDS, genital herpes... The list seems endless. So do the choices of drugs.

Over the last few years Pat and I have worked hard to earn credibility with Maui's young people. We have fed them, clothed them, gone to court with them, paid their fines, driven them to job interviews, and been there for them whenever they needed an old fart to talk to. I never know when the door will get knocked on, or when the phone is going to ring.

A week in the life of the Bottlehopper. Monday I spend two hours helping eighteen-and-under young adults with substance abuse problems. They're in a program. Wednesday, two hours with grown-ups in after-care as they return to the work force. Wednesday night is my home group, my own sick-and-sober AA meeting. Thursday is boys' night at the suite, where I have four young men over for dinner and a swim and "talking story." Friday night, we might take a couple of seventeen-year-olds out for a prime-rib dinner to celebrate a one-year clean-and-sober chip. (Who would have thought at fifty-five I'd be double-dating with teenagers?) Saturday, go canoeing with a couple of the young men. Sunday morning at nine o'clock, an AA meeting on the beach; in the afternoon we play volleyball. Bottlehopper supplies the soda pops. Afterwards, we have a swim and eats at my condo, and then we're off to the young-people's AA meeting at eight o'clock—right after Bart Simpson.

The best way to keep sober, feel happy, and fulfill the purpose of the program is to give your sobriety away. When five of those young folks completed their first three steps, Pat and I gave them and their counselor a celebration dinner at the posh Five Palms Restaurant. You should have seen them. All dressed up. I was so proud of them. Like a proud uncle.

Okay, a grandfather.

"It's an honest program, Bob."

My philosophy is simple when dealing with the young: clear boundaries work.

For example, I give out magic quarters to lots of them. The quarters are for a phone call before they use. The key word is "before." Or, if they are done with their relapse and want a ride to treatment, fine. But I refuse to waste my time talking to anyone still using. It's as simple and as complicated as that.

Maybe that's "tough love." Certainly it's self-preservation for the Bottlehopper.

Last year, we knew that when we got back to Edmonton, we were going skiing at our timeshare in Panorama. We have a three-bedroom-with-loft, and it's right on the ski hill.

So I decided that I wanted to make an offer. After talking it over with Pat, I announced that if any of the five wanted to create half the air fare and one hundred dollars spending money, I'd provide a ski-trip to the Canadian Rockies. Pat and I would pay for the skiing.

I presented the idea to Diane, a dedicated Castle counselor. She thought it was a great and generous offer.

Right away, two boys got promises of help from their parents and said they were coming with us. Suddenly the situation was scary—what with the inherent danger involved in skiing. To be totally honest, I had some major concerns about my liability for one, a juvenile, if he were injured. This was a realistic fear. I am not just another pretty face, and the thought of a Hawaiian family suing me for everything that I own did not intrigue me. We vented our concerns with the boy's mom. She agreed to sign a notarized waiver of liability.

Business is business. I didn't just fall off the turnip truck.

To further our protection we also paid for extra medical insurance. Just to be safe.

About a week later, out of the blue, twenty-three-year-old Jeff asked if he could come, too. He's a great guy, sober and straight for five years, has his own carpet-cleaning business, and can afford to pay for his airfare. Naturally we said yes. We were happy to have him along. His buddy and roommate, Ben, one of our favorites, accepted our offer to come as our guest. Ben is fighting the good fight.

In all, we had four with us at Panorama.

All they had to do was ski from our back door to the Toby chair, cut over to the quad chair, and then the whole mountain was at their disposal—a five-thousand-foot vertical drop. Two of our young guests had never been "off the rock"—that is, away from Maui. Only one of them had ever been in snow, and that had been when he was really young.

"Shoots" is a pidgin expression that means "super."

Trying to do some good. We do these things because we choose to, because we still can.

We scurried around getting tickets paid for and buying extra medical insurance for all four young men. The great Canadian adventure was set to go. Charge!

We did the magnificent West Edmonton Mall. The water park, the bungy jump, the ice skating, the video arcade...What a ball-buster of a time we had. Enough laughter to last a lifetime.

The memory of that island kid building his first snowball, and the look of the devil before he threw it at me. The laughter when I tackled him down in retaliation. I taught him how a face-washing in snow feels. We made angels by lying on our backs and waving our arms and legs.

He had to pull me up. I'm a turtle when I get flat on my back.

The next morning, the mountain. Formidable. The boys and their enthusiasm. Coming down out of control on their rears, ears, and elbows. The re-telling of the day's adventures in the hot tub. Seeing them struggle to stay awake until nine o'clock. Trips to Fairmont and Radium's outdoor hot spring pools. Eating those big fluffy Canadian snowflakes as we sat in the hot pool. Such memories.

The strained silence of the ride to the airport on their departure. The poignant statement: "Bob and Pat, these have been the best fourteen days of my whole life." He's fifteen, sober and clean for seven months and five days.

Receiving Ben and Jeff's thank-you card. "We will treasure this trip forever..."

I suppose it's okay to dream. What if this book is a success?

Imagine putting a generous percentage of the net into a trust fund for cultural exchange between Canadian and American young people who are recovering from chemical dependency. Perhaps a scholarship fund for continuing education. Funds to help acquire knowledge. Knowledge is power. Growth gives strength.

Giving something back is a sure way to keep what you have.

John McCrae, a Canadian doctor, wrote a poem during the first world war called "In Flanders Fields." Doctor McCrae was killed in one of those insane "over the top" charges into machine-gun fire, tending to the wounded. The poem is a poignant plea to stop the insanity. Unless we do, they who died have suffered in vain.

The road to recovery from chemical dependency is littered with the tombstones of those who didn't make it.

To you from failing hands we throw
The torch; be yours to hold it high.
If ye break faith with us who die
We shall not sleep, though poppies grow
In Flanders fields.

I hope the torch that this old dude passes will be held high by those I touch, and that it will be passed on to all those yet to come. I want to finish with the Serenity Prayer, the prayer that I heard at Mister Tyler's funeral a lifetime ago:

God, grant me the serenity to accept the things I cannot change, the courage to change the things I can, and the wisdom to know the difference.

Amen.

Afterword: Frequently Asked Questions

How did normal people treat you when you were a practicing skid-row alcoholic?

First, I really have some difficulty with the word "normal." Methinks the term is a grossly over rated. Who decides what's normal? What's the benchmark? Do normal people chose the criteria for being normal? Is that fair?

To answer the spirit of the question, though, I was treated with pity, disgust, and contempt. Sometimes with anger.

When people expressed pity, it was pretty simple to manipulate them into giving me a free smoke or, better still, some cash for booze. They would always say, "Be sure to get something to eat." Yeah, sure.

Disgust can also be used to score money. Sometimes disgusted people would give me money just to get me to go away. Same thing with the cold-contempt type. These people don't like to be embarrassed. No one does.

Panhandling is an acquired survival skill. You learn to pick out the different types of "normal" people. I became adept at the art. But I had to beware the "normal" person who was angry.

You never knew why he was angry. Maybe his dad drank too much, beat his mom, abused him and his sister, or did all three. Perhaps a drunken uncle had given it to him up the ass. All these are valid reasons for anger. But none of it was my doing.

Surviving his anger, though, was my problem.

These "drunk bashers" are in the same category as "gay bashers"—sick bastards. They are not "normal." These sociopaths seem to travel in packs that gather around an aggressive-dominant leader. You just have to avoid these sickos, or you won't survive for long.

That's why drunks learn to be territorial. I tried to stay under a measure of control until I entered the sanctuary of the flop. Then I could drink myself into nirvana. The down side to nirvana is that you become extremely vulnerable to these individuals. So you want to pass out in a safe place.

Trouble is, as I progressed in my vocation, my tolerance for alcohol became fickle. Some days, what used to be enough was way too much. I would lose control, get too inebriated, and then I'd be vulnerable.

I heard many first-hand accounts of beatings and hospitalizations. The assaults were always vicious and totally random—just the wrong place at the wrong time. The drunks weren't even robbed, just beaten, given broken ribs, stitches, concussions, serious beatings.

Perhaps you've read in the newspaper about these animals torching a drunk, using lighter fluid or some other flammable, sometimes watching him burn to death. Random—like what happened when Michael Jordan's father died at the rest stop in Florida. Someone was going to die, and he just happened to be there. Stories like that fill my with gut fear.

How was your sex life on the skids?

I was a real loser. Liquor enhances my desire but taketh away my performance.

I used the services of prostitutes if I were flush. I just didn't have time or desire to establish meaningful relationships. If I didn't get laid soon after I got into town, I just ended up yanking on it till it felt good. That's the way it was.

I got crotch critters once, twice, or thrice. Also got the clap a couple of times. (No applause was involved.) If memory serves me, a discharge and burning when urinating were the symptoms. A shot of penicillin and a prescription of antibiotics worked for that. Blue ointment and a pubic shave worked for the crotch critters. I'm not referring to Dungeness crabs here.

Sometimes on the skids I also got involved with what we called colloquially "coyotes." Here's why. As the evening progresses, the females in the bar start to look a lot better. The drunker you get, the better they look. Broken, crooked noses become interesting features. Scars become beauty marks. Toothlessness becomes a sign of character. Obesity becomes more to make love to.

And then you wake up nude in a hotel room three or four hours later. Her head is resting on your arm and she is blissfully snoring. It's a coin-toss which one of you pissed the bed.

In the harsh light of day she invariably looks brutal. But if you move your arm, she'll wake up. You're trapped. The only way out is to chew your arm off.

That's why they call them "coyotes."

Gingerly you lift the covers and ask your special purpose if he did anything. You hope to God that you only passed out. But a stiff cock has no conscience.

In stealthy silence you extricate yourself and slip into your clothes. Because you're a gentleman, you lock the door behind you. Then you realize where you are. She's in your room.

How the hell are you going to get rid of her now? Conceive a story for the desk man. You were just being kind—something about giving her a place to sleep for the night—and would the desk man please extricate her for you? "Wait about an hour," you say. That will give you a head start.

Of course, I was no prize either. Wonder what the girls called the experience of waking up next to something like me. Perhaps a Bob-a-yote.

Let's not forget that these adventures took place in those magical days before AIDS, genital herpes, and the like. AIDS is a tough way to lose weight. Thanks again for saving my sorry ass, God!

What about your friends and family? Didn't they try to help you?

Fact is, I didn't feel worthy of help. I didn't deserve it. I was consumed by guilt over my failure as a husband and father.

False pride!

Not only that, I simply disappeared off the face of the planet. I believe I was registered as a missing person. I ditched my identification and became a persona non grata. I survived by my wits, and I'm not stupid. So I was able to remain hidden for quite some time.

My mother died while I was on the skids. Just another skeleton in my closet full of bones. My God, did those bones ever rattle at three in the morning when I couldn't sleep! In recovery, I had to study every rib and fossil. So many to whom I had to make amends. I set out to make a list of everyone I would contact and apologize to. You should try it. It was a difficult task, but it got easier when I took a wise man's advice and put at the top of the list my own name.

What's it like for you today not being able to drink at social gatherings? How do normal people react to your not drinking? What do you do when everyone else is drinking?

Well, more often than not it's a blessing. The turd instinct—make that the herd instinct—still prevails. We all want to be accepted by our peers as equals. As in the ugly duckling yarn—no one likes to be seen as different.

Usually, I politely say, "I am coasting, thank you."

Sometimes I just say, "No thank you."

I try: "I'm pretty off-the-wall when I'm sober..."

Rarely do I have to say firmly, "I choose not to drink!" Rarer still is the need to be rude and say, "It's none of your fucking business why I choose not to drink!"

In fact, it's amazing that I hardly ever say the word "fuck" any more.

No matter what I say, though, I can sense a sinister attitude looming in the subconscious of many drinkers. Why isn't this guy having a drink? Is he weird? Is he some kind of spy? Is his wife forcing him to refuse drinks?

I've even had these poor misguided souls switch my drink to one with booze in it. Sometimes they wouldn't tell me. Sometimes they'd say, "I slipped a double shot of vodka in your Pepsi, Bob, so Pat won't know." (By the way, the old ploy of drinking vodka so no one will smell the booze—that's a real joke. Even if you don't smell like a brewery, your inability to walk or talk will invite speculation.) The poor souls just wanted to help me loosen up, get more sociable. They were just being kind.

Please be careful when you're pouring drinks. Some recovering alcoholics take a prescribed drug called anabuse. If those people drink, their livers refuse to process the booze. They could die.

Generally speaking, I have to be wary—not paranoid, just wary—in social situations.

Try being wary yourself sometime. It's most instructive. Dare to stay sober and observe the behavior of those you respect. Watch them change and start performing. Listen to your role models become loud and opinionated about nothing, yelling at each other in trivial, no-sense conversations. Observe the antics. Some turn into bantam roosters who want to take on the world. Some get emotional and cry in their beer. The vocabulary grows more and more colorful. The content of the conversation becomes an affront to your audio appendages. Stay sober, if you dare, and listen to the gibberish. For me, it's a funny, sad experience.

I prefer to avoid these situations.

When you entertain in your own home, do you serve drinks? Do you keep alcohol in your home?

Yes is the answer to both questions.

A word of caution here. Keeping booze in my home—that works for me. But I don't recommend this practice for anyone else with an alcohol problem. In point of fact, I would discourage keeping alcohol in your home. It's not snakes and ladders, this disease of alcoholism. If you're not completely comfortable in your sobriety, don't have alcohol around and don't hang around alcohol. Why take unnecessary chances?

But I feel more comfortable having it around.

I remember in the beginning feeling very mixed-up about not drinking. Insecure. I used to hang around bars and drink soda pop. "If you sleep with dogs, you get fleas, Bob."

I also poured drinks like a bloody idiot. The mind-set was: I'll pour ridiculously strong drinks for you. Please like me. Like me at any cost, even though I don't drink.

A bloody idiot!

Bob now serves two punches when he entertains. They are different in color. One punch has alcohol and one has none. Just to be safe, I reserve a rather distinctive glass for my personal use.

I realize that the wheels won't fall off if I take a swallow by mistake. Or will they? I err on the side of caution. I also run like hell if I feel uncomfortable.

My sobriety is the foundation of my entire life. My sobriety comes even before my relationship with Pat. All that I hold dear and love would be gone—me, too.

What are the danger signs of problem drinking? How can you tell?

You don't have to be an expert to spot the problem drinkers. It's not nuclear physics.

Problem drinkers usually have profound behavior changes. The quiet personalities become loud and argumentative. The loud ones become quiet or sullen. Church-going women start dancing provocatively on the tables. Respectable men start arguing when their wives insist on driving home. People stop listening but keep talking. Most are consistent in their behavior—each time they drink, they put on a performance. The routine loss of control in social situations is a red flag.

We accept this type of behavior because these folks are usually such great people when sober.

Notice the people who are still drinking with resolve when the food is being served. Some may gulp their drinks. Others drink doubles. Most drink with a purpose.

Sometimes these problem drinkers can't work the next day. They have their wives phone the office to say they have the flu. Canadians call this the "twenty-six-ounce flu" because our fifths are twenty-six ounces. My advice to the wife would be stop doing the phoning for him. You're only enabling him to continue.

Many of these functioning problem drinkers manage to keep from crossing over the line to chronic alcoholism. Usually, it's just shithouse luck if they do. Fortunately, some suffer enormous hangovers and terrible headaches—especially when their wives tell them how they behaved last night—so they tend to limit their drinking to binges. Have two doubles before you get out of bed. That's how a binge gets started. Worked great for me!

Guilt sometimes helps problem drinkers hold the line. It can be sobering to find out that you goosed your boss's wife, and then afterwards tried to do the same to your top saleswoman. Nice going, asshole.

I find that kind of behavior painful to observe, and I try to avoid seeing it. They know not what they are tempting. Usually we arrive early and leave early so that we're spared most of the shenanigans.

Do you ever get thirsty?

Yes, I can become vulnerable. Usually it's because I haven't been to a meeting that week. No one said sobriety was going to be easy.

Problem-solving is a strength with me, but I can only handle three significant crises at a time. When I get into that much pressure, I call a friend or get to a meeting. The AA program is my security blanket.

The length of a person's sobriety isn't relevant. That little voice of insanity in the cortex of your brain can still talk to you. My advice: do not listen. The worst day sober is better than the best day drinking.

What tricks do you use to stay sober?

I sacrifice a goat every full moon, then read the entrails of a chicken...Bob, you are a sarcastic bastard.

I go to a minimum of two meetings a week. I have a sponsor, my Sensei, with whom I can ventilate honestly. And I'm involved almost daily in helping other recovering alcoholics stay sober.

I want to pass the torch of sobriety to as many as I can. My *raison d'etre* is to work with young people in recovery from substance abuse. I have a gift for communicating with them. I care. So does my partner in life, Pat. We are a team.

One more thing.

I guess it's not macho to say this, but here it goes. Every morning when I wake up, I ask for help facing the day's challenges. I turn my will and my life over to a person greater than myself. I call this person God. This old gray-haired dude is also smart enough to say thanks at night. Aside from that, my religious beliefs are private, and I choose to keep them that way.

Why did you become an alcoholic?

Actually it was a fluke. I woke up one day a heavy-drinking successful businessman—a young lion in the real estate profession with a wife, son, home, and new car—and I left for work. On the way, I made a mistake. I turned right instead of left, and I woke up about three years later living under a bridge on skid row. I had crossed over the invisible line that separates the functioning alcoholic from the chronic.

Quite simply, the drink took the man.

There's no "off" switch for alcoholism, folks. It's progressive and usually terminal. The only way to quit is to STOP DRINKING COMPLETELY. Give up! Go on to something else!

I feel no sympathy for the practicing drunk, and that's a tough-love reality. I have been there and done that. If you want, in fact, you can put the demon back in the bottle. I did. But it's not easy. You have to want sobriety more than you want the drink that straightens you out in the morning, when you're sick and shaking and every nerve in your body is screaming for a cure.

The chosen few get and stay sober. If you want my help, call me. But call me before you drink, not after. I don't have much success talking with practicing alcoholics, so I chose not to.

That's a matter of self-preservation.

Why did I become an alcoholic? Perhaps the following litany will help explain. I didn't write it, but I've adapted it from an anonymous newspaper clipping. The author obviously knew what he was talking about.

> *I drank because I had the right, and everything in my life went wrong.*
> *I drank to help me cope, and I became a failure.*
> *I drank to feel numb and felt guilt.*
> *I drank to sleep and awoke un-rested and hung-over.*
> *I drank to feel comfortable socially and became anti-social, a recluse*
> *I drank to stimulate my intellect and suffered blackouts.*
> *I drank to be sophisticated and became obnoxious.*
> *I drank to be accepted and ended up scorned.*
> *I drank to forget and became haunted by my past.*
> *I drank because I was thirsty, and a thousand drinks didn't quench my obsession for more.*
> *I drank to escape myself, but I always ended up back alone, stuck with me.*
> *I drank because I hated God.*
> *After much struggle, I understood.*

Because, because.

I have nothing more to say about because. My focus in recovery is being sober for today. Being the best I can for today. Helping one person in recovery today. I cannot change even one second of the past.

Sure, I check the rear-view mirror often, but my focus is forward. Those who choose to forgive me are wonderful, compassionate human beings. I can accept and live with those who do not.

Funny thing, though—no one ever apologized to me about any of their own behaviors. Perhaps they feel some guilt, too. You yourself may be somewhat self-righteous in your judgment of me. For my part, the dead will bury the dead. The past is an exercise in futility. I'm having too much fun wallowing in the present.

In closing, a question to you from the Bottlehopper:

How do you, my reader, feel about drinking?

Perhaps your answer would be, "The demon of drink causes the mind to be poisoned, ruins families, stimulates crime, pollutes the brain, and drains our social system. I vote against drinking alcohol."

You could also reply that alcohol is "God's gift that gladdens the heart, the protection against winter's cold, the sedative that helps us to embrace Morpheus, the essence of Thanksgiving and Christmas, the main component of any social gathering, and, most of all, the cash cow that puts tax money into the hands of the poor and needy." Then you would perhaps be emphatically in favor of drinking.

Your answer could be both. Ethyl is a two-sided coin. There is no wrong answer. Just treat alcohol with respect and I will sleep better.

Perhaps, like me, you have noticed a change in public beliefs about drinking. During the sixties and seventies, I drank like what we called the police—a pig. Now, hope is exemplified in a young friend called Jeff. He's an American who lives on the island of Maui. Just twenty-three, he has over six years clean and sober.

Jeff, you're an inspiration—a lighthouse in the turbulent sea of recovery. Go for it, pal. Keep a firm grip on the rudder of your sobriety.

Keep Going on . . . Going

Zooz! Bob, boB, and the Bottlehopper are still alive and well. Not many would have "made book" on this fact. Hell, I wouldn't have "made book" on it. January 2001 finds us on Maui reviewing the first year of the new millennium. The boB of active addiction is in remission, one grateful day at a time.

A competent driver focuses a considerable amount of time looking in his rearview mirror, just checking for potential problems. I have learned to do the same at the end of each calendar year. The months December and January are devoted to enthusiastically reviewing the previous year. This review leads me into the critical goal setting process for the new year. Asking positive questions about how I could have done something better. Handled a crisis with a different expertise, or asked for advice. Perhaps more information gathering and research could be implemented before making decisions. Being an active member of two 12 step fellowships my mandate is to practice the principals of my recovery in all my affairs.

The criteria for this review exercise is commitment, the right attitude, and rigorous honesty. Bottlehopper's a believer, setting goals does work. Did you know if you confidently expect to be successful, ya will be. No matter what. If one programs successful, positive thoughts into your mental computer that's what unfolds in your life. If you are what you think you are ? 90% of the time you will be. So think good stuff. Positive programing produces positive results. The glass is always half full. The benefit of this comprenhesive review is manifested in the goal setting process for the new year. The key to setting goals is writing them down. Goals that aren't written are wishes. Those that don't have clear written goals are forever condemned to work for those that do. Perhaps if New Year's resolutions were written we would do better with them.

Six really significant events came to pass in the first year of the new millineum. Accepting life, on lifes terms, is a continuing challenge of my recovery. Facing reality hasn't been one of my strong suites. Using alcohol and drugs to numb myself from experiencing unpleasnt feelings was almost my demise. Things really do seem to happen around me though. Nothing about my life is boring. Most importantly the bottlehopper was able to bank another year clean and sober. Everything else pivots on my continued recovery. Being clean and sober, is the fulcrum of my life.

While on Maui, in the fall of 1999, Pat, the light of my life had a heart attack and was emergency airlifted to Oahu where an angiogram and angioplasty was done. She began her recovery in Maui and continued to recover when we arrived back in Edmonton. Then, before we came back to Maui in October of 2000, Pat had to have emergency triple bypass surgery. More things are wrought by prayer than this world dreams of. I was home for the operation and when she started her rehabilitation, but, because my nephew Sean and a buddy were coming to Maui to visit, I had to be there. Feeling guilty, I flew to Maui with Sean and Carlos. Pat had no problem with me leaving her in Edmonton. She said, "I have enough on my plate without having you there as a distraction." I can be a handfull, sometimes, two handfulls. Even in recovery. My squeeze didn't get medical clearance to join me on Maui until January 15, 2001. To expedite her rehab, we did lots of walking on the beach, and of course this isn't hard work on Maui. The scenery is spectacular.

The second most important woman in my life, Tricia, our daughter, was married on September 16, 2000. At center ice, no less, in the Sky Reach Center where the Edmonton Oilers play professional hockey. We walked out to center ice on red carpets. Four bridesmaids and escorts, best man and maid of honor, flower girl, ring bearer, and 2 pipers. The bride's close relatives in the home penalty box, the grooms in the visitor's sin bin. Over 300 guests attended the wedding ceremony. Tricia's nuptials were blessed by perfect weather. Some of the wedding pictures were taken in our backyard which has world class landscaping. Our Japanese Garden is complete with a Koi pond and makes a wonderful background for pictures. The wedding party of girls slept over at the family home the night before. I made green and red banana pancakes for breakfast. Just like when Trish was in school and had pajama parties. A little food coloring makes them unique. Tricia specially requested them for her last single breakfast. So many warm memories. We are truly blessed with Tricia. I love her and just as important like and respect her. Les, our son-in-law too.

Last spring the old fart bought a new Yamaha 1100cc. motorcycle and rode his hog through the Rocky Mountains to Vancouver. I went alone on this adventure of some 2500 miles. At 57, I am finally growing up. Not even afraid of being by myself anymore. It was a hoot. Scary, shivery, and spectacular, describe the trip. Skinny dipping in lakes just off the highway. Not having an agenda. Sleeping under the stars, wind chill, rain, and a profound sense of freedom are part of the motorcycle experience. Sure it's dangerous riding a motorcycle. The "being on the edge" component of my personality is alive and well. Please believe me when I say that the motorcycle isn't part of any male menopause. Do I protest too much? Death Wish? More a celebration of life methinks. I visited a bunch of old friends, while I was on the coast. One of them is a provincial judge. Was the look in their eyes all astonishment, admiration, disbelief? Could some of the looks been pride in my accomplishment? Acknowledgement of my recovery, attitude of living life to its fullest every day. Perhaps even a little envy?

Finally, after getting Tricia married off and becoming a free man, I adopted Julian in December of 2000. My prince is a 17 year old young adult in recovery, and lives on Maui. We have known Julian since he was a pukey 13 year old. He is a handsome black Hawaiian American. Julian looks a bit like a young Muhammed Ali. My prince has been in and out of foster homes and in recovery programs as long as we have known him. He is a bright young man with a high IQ. When Julian returns home after completing a drug and alcohol program, life falls apart for him. His mom uses prescription pills and drinks. The last time I was at his mom's house two police cars and an ambulance were there. I had received an emotional call for help and responded. When you have me for a friend you're stuck with me. I even visit you in hospital.

His mom had either slipped or fallen and had possibly cracked her ribs. She maintained Julian had pushed her. I explained to the police that if I were given the ok from Julian's mom, with them as witnesses, he could come to Kihei and stay with me. Julian's mom was going to go to the hospital for X rays. Poof, no problem, no paperwork, a solution. Maui's finest acquiesed. This ongoing problem with Julian's mom and Julian was well known to the police. A "no win" situation. The next day I explained my fears for Julian, and his mom's safety to his social worker. Kim agreed, and the wheels were put in motion. First we got a power of attorney for Julian, legally executed. A new son at my age?

Julian will have to make some very important choices this year. Where he wants to go to college, yes, he does have the smarts to attend university. Julian and I had a big time sit down pow-wow. He knows when I get screwed I like to be kissed. Sure honesty, trust and mutual respect are our ultimate goals. For now clear boundaries are in place. I messed up somewhat. Call me a "doubting Bob". I'll explain the conversation, "If you expect me to buck up for your education, show me some production scholastically this semester." Julian responded with a 96.2 average. "Ye men of little faith" comes to mind. So I have been taking him to teen dances, surfing, 12 step meetings, sporting events, dates with his girlfriend. I have returned to being a human taxi cab, just like with my own kids. The glass is always half full. My prince is learning how to drive, a standard shift no less. This spring after graduation he attends a 6 week course at Upward Bound. Julian has been in this excellent program for 3 years. Upward bound prepares the high school student for university. Then he comes to Alberta for the summer. Perhaps he and I will redo my motorcycle trip to the coast. Quality time, male bonding, for Julian and I. More importantly we can set some goals for his future.

Good grief, I'm pushing the hell out of sixty. Where this road I have chosen to take with Julian goes, I have no idea. I do have faith though. Faith in my higher power. Faith in my 12 step program. I have been less than a success as a father with my stepson and son. Perhaps this is an opportunity God has given me to do better with Julian.

In conclusion this spring we have 4 more young adults from Maui coming home with us for 2 weeks. We have had over 15 young people in recovery share West Edmonton Mall, bungy jump, waterpark, rollercoaster, Drop of Doom, ice skate, cosmic bowl, paint ball... They have also shared Panorama Resort in the Canadian Rockies for a weeks snow boarding. Imagine the 7 hour flight to Edmonton. Some of these kids have never been off the rock. This is the 4th annual great Canadian vacation. So Bottlehopper will keep trudging along the happy road of destiny. Content with living life in the moment, to its fullest, every day my higher power gives me. Sort of like the energizer Bunny. Bottlehopper keeps going and going...Perhaps a future book project would be to write an update on the young addicts/alcoholics who have have shared their recovery with me...That would be a hoot!